T0211354

High-Quality Illumination of Virtual Objects Based on an Environment Estimation in Mixed Reality Applications

Tobias Schwandt

High-Quality Illumination of Virtual Objects Based on an Environment Estimation in Mixed Reality Applications

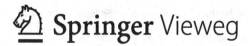

Springer Vieweg

Tobias Schwandt
Computer science and Automation
Ilmenau University of Technology
Ilmenau, Germany

PhD Thesis, Technische Universität Ilmenau, 2021

ISBN 978-3-658-35191-5   ISBN 978-3-658-35192-2   (eBook)
https://doi.org/10.1007/978-3-658-35192-2

Responsible Editor: Stefanie Eggert
This Springer Vieweg imprint is published by the registered company Springer Fachmedien
Wiesbaden GmbH part of Springer Nature.
The registered company address is: Abraham-Lincoln-Str. 46, 65189 Wiesbaden, Germany

"Anything that happens, happens."

— Adams, Douglas, The Hitchhiker's Guide to the Galaxy

Acknowledgment

This thesis has been created over a long period on a long road. On this way, different people have made an important contribution to it—directly and indirectly. This includes intensive discussions and feedback as well as general support during difficult parts while writing the thesis. I would like to briefly mention a few people who have had a great impact on the approaches in this thesis.

First, I would like to mention Wolfgang Broll as my supervisor, professor at the Ilmenau University of Technology and head of the group for Virtual Worlds and Digital Games. A few years ago, he hired me and gave me the opportunity to start my thesis. During my time at the research group, I was constantly supported to define my research field. The time was characterized by regular meetings to discuss the current state of research and how to continue. He was always open-minded for new and innovative topics with constructive criticism of the work, the publications, and the next steps. Even besides regular meetings, the office door was always open. Many thanks Wolfgang for your support.

In addition to Wolfgang Broll, my colleagues Florian Weidner and Christian Kunert were outstanding companions. Both are also research assistants at the research group and pursue the goal of the thesis. Together we talked a lot about our research, exchanged new information and supported each other. We wrote several papers and defined ourselves in the research world. It is nice to be able to say that a private friendship has developed beyond work, which will hopefully continue for many years and many more papers. Florian and Christian—thank you for your feedback, hints, support, and for the heartfelt laughter we had together.

Moreover, I would like to thank two other people who played an important role: my second reviewer Beat Brüderlin from the Ilmenau University of Technology and the third reviewer, Thorsten Grosch from the Clausthal University of Technology. Collaboration and meetings were helpful and always productive. Thank you for supporting this thesis and the research.

On my way to the final submission, other people also contributed an important part, which does not concern the content. At this point I would like to thank my family and in particular, my wife Karoline. She is always by my side and accompanied me on sometimes winding streets. Since she is a research assistant herself, we were able to complement and support each other well. I love you!

I am pleased that this first big step in the research world was taken together. *Thank you.*

Abstract

Visualizations of virtual objects in the real environment is often done by a simplified representation with simple surfaces and without reference to the surrounding environment. The seamless fusion of the virtual and real environment is, however, an essential factor in many areas, which is of particular importance when calculating lighting in mixed realities on mobile devices. Current approaches focus on approximations, which allow the calculation of diffuse lighting, whereby the rendering of glossy reflection properties is often neglected.

The aim of this thesis is to enable the visualization of mirror-like reflective surfaces in mixed reality. In order to achieve this goal, various approaches are explored enabling high-quality visualization of virtual objects in realtime with a focus on the use of common hardware such as cameras, sensors in mobile devices, and partially depth sensors. The first approach uses the current camera image to reconstruct 360-degree lighting by transforming the current camera image directly onto a cubemap in each frame. On top of this approach, the technique is enhanced by stitching the current camera image in combination with the position and rotation to estimate a 360-degree lighting. Uncaptured parts by the camera are filled with semantic inpainting using a neural network. In this way, complete ambient lighting can be estimated, which enables detailed reflections. The results provide a novel way to embed complex and simple geometric shapes with glossy surfaces in the real world which, in contrast to existing approaches, offers a higher level of detail in the reflections without using additional hardware. All approaches are designed to be used on mobile devices which provides new opportunities for the different use cases and areas of application for modern mixed reality.

Kurzfassung

Die Visualisierung virtueller Objekte in der Realität erfolgt bei vielen Anwendungen oftmals durch eine vereinfachte Darstellung ohne Bezug zur umliegenden Umgebung. Dabei ist die nahtlose Verschmelzung der virtuellen und realen Umgebung in vielen Bereichen ein wesentlicher Faktor, der insbesondere bei der Beleuchtungsberechnung in gemischten Realitäten von großer Bedeutung ist. Aktuelle Ansätze legen den Fokus auf Approximationen, welche eine Berechnung der diffusen Beleuchtung ermöglichen, wobei die Darstellung glänzender Beleuchtungseigenschaften vernachlässigt wird.

Das Ziel dieser Arbeit ist eine Visualisierung von spiegelnden Oberflächen in erweiterten Realitäten zu ermöglichen. Um dieses Ziel zu erreichen werden verschiedene Verfahren aufgezeigt, die eine hochwertige Darstellung virtueller Objekte in Echtzeit ermöglichen, wobei der Fokus auf der Verwendung üblicher Hardware wie Kameras, Sensoren in mobilen Endgeräten und teilweise Tiefensensoren liegt. Das erste Verfahren verwendet das aktuelle Kamerabild zur Rekonstruktion einer 360-Grad Beleuchtung durch die Transformation des Bildes auf eine Würfelkarte. Anschließend wird dieser Ansatz durch ein Stitching erweitert, bei dem das aktuelle Bild zusammen mit der Position und Rotation der Kamera genutzt wird, um eine Umgebungsbeleuchtung zu erstellen. Dabei von der Kamera nicht erfasste Bereiche werden durch ein semantisches Inpainting, basierend auf einem neuronalen Netz, aufgefüllt. Hierdurch kann das komplette Umgebungslicht approximiert werden, welches die Darstellung detaillierter Reflexionen ermöglicht. Die Ergebnisse der Ansätze zeigen neuartige Möglichkeiten, geometrische Formen mit glänzenden Oberflächen in die reale Umgebung einzubetten und bietet im Vergleich zu bestehenden Methoden einen höheren Detailgrad in den Reflexionen. Alle Ansätze sind für eine Verwendung auf mobilen Endgeräten konzipiert, wodurch neue Möglichkeiten für verschiedene Einsatz- und Anwendungsbereiche der erweiterten Realität existieren.

Contents

Abbreviations

AO	Ambient Occlusion
API	Application Programming Interface
AR	Augmented Reality
BRDF	Bidirectional Reflection Distribution Function
BTF	Bidirectional Texture Function
CNN	Convolution Neural Network
DVCT	Delta Voxel Cone Tracing
FIS	Filtered Importance Sampling
FoV	Field of View
FPS	Frame per Second
FXAA	Fast Approximate Anti-Aliasing
GAN	Generative Adversarial Network
GI	Global Illumination
GIF	Guided Image Filter
GLSL	OpenGL Shading Language
GPU	Graphical Processing Unit
GUI	Graphical User Interface
HCB	Hierarchical Color Buffer
HDR	High Dynamic Range
HDRI	High Dynamic Range Image
HMD	Head Mounted Display
IBL	Image-Based Lighting
IOR	Index Of Refraction
ISM	Imperfect Shadow Map
LDR	Low Dynamic Range
LDRI	Low Dynamic Range Image

LUT	Lookup Texture
MR	Mixed Reality
NDF	Normal Distribution Function
PBR	Physically Based Rendering
PDF	Probability Density Function
ReLU	Rectified Linear Unit
RNM	Reoriented Normal Mapping
RSM	Reflective Shadow Map
SDK	Software Development Kit
SFM	Structure From Motion
SH	Spherical Harmonics
SLAM	Simultaneous Localization and Mapping
SMAA	(Enhanced) Subpixel Morphological Anti Aliasing
SSAO	Screen Space Ambient Occlusion
SSDO	Screen Space Directional Occlusion
SSR	Screen Space Reflections
SURF	Speeded Up Robust Features
TSDF	Truncated Signed Distance Function
VCT	Virtual Cone Tracing
VR	Virtual Reality

List of Algorithms

List of Figures

List of Tables

Introduction

1

The seamless fusion of real and virtual content has inspired people for a long time. Most of the ideas were declared as science fiction in the literature but have become real in recent years. Technologies like mobile phones, computers, robots, or artificial intelligence are part of our daily life. These technologies offer the possibility to see and interact with the world differently. One of these emerging technologies is Augmented Reality (AR) which enhances the real world by embedding virtual objects into it. It is a sub-area of Mixed Reality (MR) which also includes other variants of visual perception through digital content like augmented virtuality [80].

Today, MR is widely used in many different areas to support our daily life and workflow. Major players such as Facebook, Apple, Microsoft or Google push forward MR or MR-related technologies. Almost every day, new applications and approaches are published. Some of these applications allow for annotation of objects, place 3D objects on the ground, collaborative scanning of the spatial environment, or estimating objects and storing them in the ARCloud—a collaborative environment in parallel to the real world. Different areas like entertainment, live broadcasting, education, design, or medicine use MR nowadays. Each of these areas and applications expand the real world with virtual content often aiming for realistic visualization. In some applications, the goal is to minimize the visual difference between real world and virtual content, which is examined in more detail in this thesis.

1.1 Motivation

The purpose of this thesis is to emphasize novel algorithms for the high-quality and plausible rendering of virtual objects within the real world. According to Azuma, in AR, "[…] it would appear to the user that the virtual and real objects coexisted in the same space, […]" [5], and provide the following three main characteristics:

© The Author(s), under exclusive license to Springer Fachmedien Wiesbaden GmbH, part of Springer Nature 2021
T. Schwandt, *High-Quality Illumination of Virtual Objects Based on an Environment Estimation in Mixed Reality Applications*,
https://doi.org/10.1007/978-3-658-35192-2_1

- AR is interactive or realtime,
- it is registered in 3D, and
- combines real and virtual world.

To enable advanced AR/MR applications, a coherent fusion of virtual and real objects is essential. There are two different types of coherence which need to be addressed: (1) spatial coherence and (2) visual coherence. Spatial coherence is archived by the registration and tracking of the surrounding. Nowadays, registration and tracking are usually fast, stable, and realtime-capable by relying on different sensors and software approaches. Visual coherence is realized by a sophisticated rendering of virtual objects respecting the environment. The light and geometry of the environment have to be taken into account to enable high-quality photometric registration in MR. Thus, the environment has to be digitally available in a certain way to be used for rendering—which is mostly predefined, estimated, or captured using different tools. This thesis examine different problems by asking the question: *To which extent may a seamless integration of visual content into the real environment be achieved for AR?*

Regarding the question, the following problems are the core challenges handled by the thesis:

Visual Coherence: The visualization of virtual objects in AR is significant because it is the entry point for the user to be in a mixed reality world. Here, the user's perception of an application is on high importance, which is generally made possible by a sufficient visual coherence. Many applications require seamless integration with a barely recognizable blending of real and virtual content.

Depending on the desired output quality, the rendering of high-quality images is a challenging task in the field of computer graphics. Rendering in MR is more complicated than in pure graphics applications because of different constraints like the lighting within the real world, the spatial influence between both worlds, or the rendering performance of the mobile hardware. Many modern AR applications use more light-weighted rendering approaches like comic looks or non-shiny materials for virtual objects. In comparison, movies often exhibit a high amount of visual coherence where digital content is almost indistinguishable from real objects. However, techniques for rendering virtual content in movies is usually extremely complex and therefore not suitable for realtime applications. Nowadays, different approximations can be used to enable physically-based rendering even in realtime. Modern rendering pipelines use physically-based shading approaches to create a visual output that is almost indistinguishable from reality with the capability to compute different global illumination effects.

These global illumination effects are also important for visual coherence. In particular, the specular light transport is relevant for MR. Specular lighting causes reflections, refractions, and caustics enabling the rendering of complex materials like metal or shiny plastic. This thesis addresses the visual effect of reflection by capturing the environment and rendering virtual objects using a physically-based rendering approach.

Environment Estimation: Graphics and game engines use different light sources to simulate the real-world lighting. The environment light is the major light source because it provides light incoming from all directions at a certain position. With such a light source, specular reflections on surfaces can be rendered easily. Depending on the quality of the environment texture, specular reflections can be very sharp and even allow for mirror-like surfaces. Within a MR application, the environment light is equally important but it is not easily available like in fully virtual graphics applications. Thus, the light of the environment has to be captured to enable a proper visualization of reflections.

In a fully virtual environment, the texture is captured by a virtual camera or predefined by an artist. In mixed reality, a predefined environment map is not suitable for highly realistic output because the difference between the real world and the predefinition can be too obvious which may lead to incorrect reflections on surfaces. Some approaches capture the environment map by using multiple cameras, fish-eye lenses, or other additional hardware. However, using external devices is a major drawback for the user experience because it requires additional preparation. The problem of capturing the environment is addressed in this thesis by estimating the environment with a standard mobile device and without special preparation or hardware.

Interactivity: Realtime—or interactive—frame rates are a major requirement of AR applications [5]. Fusing real and virtual content in virtual movie production has been possible for a long time. However, it is much more challenging for spatial as well as visual coherence in real-time applications.

To obtain a real-time visual coherence, the number, quality, and realism of lighting effects need to be adjusted according to the user's hardware. The visual appearance is always a trade-off between quality and available performance. Hereby, the performance of modern hardware in combination with the approximation of physically-based light transport offers the possibility to enable interactive frame rates and high-quality images. For interactive rendering, the approaches in this thesis use current generation smartphones in combination with a physically-based rendering. Moreover, the estimation of the environment lighting considers the available performance and use real-time capable solutions. So, this thesis addresses the quality of light transport by exploring new approaches for enhancing the visual coherence with the estimating of an environment map.

Geometry & Material Estimation: Besides an accurate and interactive environment estimation, a proper geometry and material estimation of the surrounding needs to be addressed. The light's interaction between surfaces of the real and virtual world needs to be considered to enable high-quality rendering of virtual objects in AR. Direct light from a light source hits a surface and the reflection of the material illuminates the surrounding geometry.

The material in the real (and virtual) world has a high influence on the behavior of the light. For example, the reflection in a simple mirror has a different influence than the reflection of a wooden table. Depending on the intensity of reflection, the surrounding objects are more or less illuminated. Thus, the rendering system needs to be aware of the geometry and material to calculate the light transport correctly.

This thesis use estimated and predefined geometry properties of the real-world environment to enable different visual effects. Moreover, the manipulation of the real world is addressed in combination with a novel rendering approach to calculate light effects like shadows on real-world surfaces.

Usability & Inclusion: The estimation of geometry, materials, and light enables a proper visual coherence in MR. Visual coherence is perceived by the user who judges the quality. However, not only visual coherence is important to have a good usability but also the user's hardware and effort for preparation. As an example, users may prefer to use common hardware like a mobile phone to have a pleasant experience without placing multiple cameras inside the room or scanning all objects to estimate material properties. Moreover, any virtual content should be available shortly after starting the application.

This thesis addresses this issue by showing novel approaches to estimate the environment with a common mobile phone. During the application lifetime, the quality of the estimation is enhanced with the help of a neural network. The presented approaches can be used to enable different light effects without the need to prepare the scene or predefine the environment map. Moreover, the approaches can also be used with different output devices that can further enhance the inclusion by using additional hardware like Head Mounted Displays (HMDs) with multiple sensors.

1.2 Contributions

The main focus of this thesis is to provide high-quality visual coherence with a real-time environment estimation. Therefore, the visual appearance is addressed by proposing a novel approach to estimate the environment lighting while relying only on a single camera image. The rendering is based on an approximation of a physically-based light transport with multiple light sources to illuminate virtual objects. One major light source is a environment light capturing the environment lighting which can be used for diffuse and specular reflections. To overcome the issue of a predefined environment lighting in MR, this thesis uses a single camera and a stitching approach in combination with a neural network. Finally, an environment light is estimated and updated in realtime to enable realistic lighting, which is filtered for diffuse and specular lighting and stored as a light probe. To render the output in realtime on mobile devices, a novel rendering is proposed which also allows a manipulation of the real world out of the box.

The problem of rendering a high-quality MR output is addressed by a graphics engine supporting Desktop PCs and Android mobile devices. During the time of research, the engine was written with different functionalities using rasterization as the main rendering pipeline with deferred rendering to enable multiple lights including directional lights, point lights, area light, and light probes. All rendering is done in High Dynamic Range (HDR) due to the importance of high-quality light transport. HDR is used inside the engine in combination with a histogram and a tone mapper converting the result for default display devices. A visual output of the engine is shown in Figure 1.1 with a virtual sphere in an open environment on sidewalk with buildings and trees around the user. The surrounding is captured during runtime and the unseen part is estimated by a neural network (parts of the sky or ceiling and the floor or pavement). The position of the sun — or main light in the scene (indoor and outdoor) — is estimated and placed accordingly to show shadows on the ground. In the reflection of the sphere in Figure 1.1, even small details like the building, trees, or cars are visible.

In summary, the main contributions of this thesis are:

- A novel approach to estimate environment lighting. Hereby, high quality specular lighting is feasible even on mirror-like surfaces.
- An approach to superimpose virtual objects on the real environment considering the lighting and geometry. All rendering and computations are done in realtime to comply with the constraints of AR.

Figure 1.1 From a video stream of a webcam or the camera of a mobile phone, the current image can be used to superimpose the real world with virtual objects. In this example, detailed information of the surroundings can be seen in the mirror-like reflection on a virtual sphere

- A novel rendering approach to combine the real and virtual world to use and even manipulate real-world geometry.

This thesis presents a realistic and physically plausible visualization in comparison to other approaches, with possible further research regarding the estimation of the environment map. The estimation of the environment light source is only the first step to estimate local light sources based on the environment map. Moreover, the environment light source can be divided regarding spatial constraints to emphasize multiple environment maps for different positions inside the real-world space. Furthermore, all the environment maps might be saved inside the ARCloud. So, many users could enhance the visualization by collaboratively capturing and estimating the real world and its properties. Based on these light probes an even more sophisticated rendering could be available for future mixed reality applications.

Scientific Publications: The results of this thesis were published in several papers. A list of papers with the highest contribution to the thesis are the following:

Tobias Schwandt and Wolfgang Broll. "A Single Camera Image Based Approach for Glossy Reflections in Mixed Reality Applications". In: *2016 IEEE International Symposium on Mixed and Augmented Reality (ISMAR)*. IEEE, 2016, pp. 37–43. Doi: https://doi.org/10.1109/ISMAR.2016.12.

Tobias Schwandt and Wolfgang Broll. "Differential G-Buffer Rendering for Mediated Reality Applications". In: *Augmented Reality, Virtual Reality, and Computer Graphics AVR 2017*. Ed. by Lucio Tommaso De Paolis, Patrick Bourdot, and Antonio Mongelli. Springer, Cham, June 2017, pp. 337–349. ISBN: 978-3-319-60928-7. DOI: https://doi.org/10.1007/978-3-319-60928-7_30.

Tobias Schwandt, Christian Kunert, and Wolfgang Broll. "Glossy Reflections for Mixed Reality Environments on Mobile Devices". In: *International Conference on Cyberworlds*. IEEE, Oct. 2018, pp. 138–143. DOI: https://doi.org/10.1109/CW.2018.00034.

Tobias Schwandt, Christian Kunert, and Wolfgang Broll. "Environment Estimation for Glossy Reflections in Mixed Reality Applications Using a Neural Network". In: *Transactions on Computational Science XXXVI: Special Issue on Cyberworlds and Cybersecurity*. Ed. by Marina L. Gavrilova, C.J. Kenneth Tan, and Alexei Sourin. Berlin, Heidelberg: Springer Berlin Heidelberg, 2020, pp. 26–42. ISBN: 978-3-662-61364-1. DOI: https://doi.org/10.1007/978-3-662-61364-1_2.

1.3 Thesis Outline

First, Chapter 1 gives a brief introduction to the topic with the basic concepts in Chapter 2. Chapter 2 also provides fundamentals to related topics and the information helpful to understand the combination of virtual and real worlds. Here, lighting and reconstruction is mainly explained in combination with MR including the current state of the art. Chapter 3 outlines novel real-time capable approaches for the plausible representation of virtual objects in the real world. This includes a spatial capturing, environment light estimation, and manipulation of the real world. The realization of the approaches to the aforementioned problems are described in Chapter 4. Based on this, Chapter 5 graphically presents the results of the approaches and their realization in order to give an impression of the various application scenarios. To highlight the real-time capability, this chapter additionally includes performance measurements. In Chapter 6, the results are discussed including limitations. Finally, a conclusion with an outlook into future work is provided in Chapter 7.

Fundamentals & State of the Art

2

The visualization of virtual objects inside the real environment is quite a complex issue and basic knowledge is required to understand the approaches in detail. Therefore, in the following the fundamentals and state of the art are described. Some parts are discussed in more detail depending on the contribution to the overall topic.

At first, some general knowledge of light transport is described in Section 2.1. This part is significant to understand the importance of light and material rendering in physically-based scenarios. The provided mathematical background can be used to render realistic lighting effects which are also used in this thesis.

Based on light transport, global illumination techniques with basic mathematics are shown in Section 2.2. This section gives a short overview into ray tracing and a more detailed look into rasterization. Ray tracing enables highly realistic outputs, but is commonly used in non-interactive setups. Thus, ray tracing is often deployed for specific effects like global illumination to enable local reflections. Besides ray tracing, rasterization is common in computer graphics for a long time, especially in realtime applications. This thesis applies rasterization for the main pipeline and the approaches — partly using ray-tracing.

Technologies related to Mixed Reality (MR) are described in Section 2.3. For a general understanding, AR, MR, and other related terminologies are described. Light estimation in mixed reality is highlighted in particular because its quality has been increased in recent AR frameworks. Therefore, the output of different light estimation types like ambient lighting or reflections is shown.

A more advanced visualization in AR is possible by embedding virtual objects in the real environment and — as already mentioned — considering the environment light. Therefore, in Section 2.4, some related techniques for reconstructing the environment with light, material, and geometry are described. Based on this reconstruction, the real environment can be partially transferred to the virtual world and a proper illumination can be created.

T. Schwandt, *High-Quality Illumination of Virtual Objects Based on an Environment Estimation in Mixed Reality Applications*, https://doi.org/10.1007/978-3-658-35192-2_2

Finally, in Section 2.5, the general concept of neural networks is described. These fundamentals are needed to understand related techniques used for the estimation of the environment. The structures and architectures of the networks are used for the approaches.

Besides the fundamentals, different mathematical equations can be found inside the thesis. Throughout the entire thesis, the notation in Table 2.1 is used.

Table 2.1 Mathematical notation of terms and formulas inside the thesis

n	normal vector
v	view vector
l	incident light vector
h	half vector
f	BRDF
f_r	specular component of BRDF
α	roughness of material
$\cdot$	dot product
$\langle \cdot \rangle$	clamped dot product

2.1   Light Transport

Light allows people to visually perceive structures — without light, the sense of sight would not exist. Accordingly, this medium is of particular importance and has been studied for many centuries. In recent years, and partly due to Albert Einstein, fundamental discoveries about light and its movement have been made. Light can be understood as particles on an electromagnetic wave whereat particles are called photons which have no mass but frequency-dependent energy.

However, light propagation is often approximated with rays in geometric optics in order to simplify the more complex calculations related to waves. Here, phenomena such as light, shadows, reflections, and refractions are easier to describe. This assumption is also the base of this thesis, wherefore the basic terms and the rendering equation is explained in more detail.

2.1.1   Photometry & Radiometry

Radiometry and photometry are related terms. Photometry describes the electromagnetic radiation in the wave range of visible light ($\sim 400nm$ to $\sim 750nm$) and is used in different applications like measurement of transmission and reflections, light sources, and astronomy. Radiometry is an extension of photometry considering the entire wavelength spectrum. Both systems usually use different units whereat each unit in one system has a corresponding term in the other system. The Table 2.2 shows the fundamental quantities essential for radiometry and photometry. Visible light is mostly used for calculations in computer graphics, wherefore the basic quantities of photometry are used in this thesis.

Table 2.2 Comparison of radiometric and photometric units. (Original by: Lagarde and Rousiers [62])

Quantity	Radiometric term	Units	Photometric term	Units
Energy	Radiant energy Q_e	Joule (J)	Luminous energy Q_v	$lm * s$
Power	Radiant flux Φ_e	$\frac{J}{s}$ or Watt (W)	Luminous flux Φ_v	Lumen (lm)
Power per solid angle	Radiant intensity I_e	$\frac{W}{sr}$	Luminous intensity I_v	$\frac{lm}{sr}$ or Candela (cd)
Power per area	Irradiance E_e	W/m^2	Illuminance E_v	$\frac{lm}{m^2}$ or Lux (lx)
Power per area per solid angle	Radiance L_e	$\frac{W}{m^2 * sr}$	Luminance L_v	$\frac{lm}{m^2 * sr}$ or Nit (nt)

2.1.2   Rendering Equation

Image synthesis is used to visualize light reflected from surfaces on a screen. Based on light information and material properties, image synthesis describes the light emerging at one point on the material. Local lighting models describe the behavior of a photon hitting a material of a surface which is either reflected, absorbed, or refracted. On very smooth surfaces, the light is completely reflected — the so-called specular reflection. All other materials split the incoming light into a reflected and refracted term. The distribution between refracted and reflected light is described later in more detail. For now it is sufficient to assume that microscopically small unevennesses of the material change the lighting by being reflected or absorbed with a certain probability. Figure 2.1 shows an example of light for rough and smooth materials.

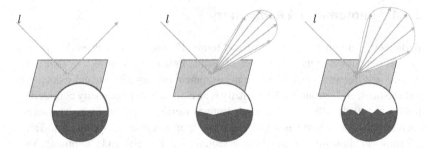

Figure 2.1 Depending on the material attributes, the incoming light rays reacts different on the surface. The material on the left side has a glossy surface while the material on the right side has a rough surface

A physically-correct calculation of the interaction between light and materials is complex because it depends on a high number of variables like polarization, phosphorescence, subsurface scattering, or fluorescence. In computer graphics, a limited number of variables are used to calculate the reflected light of a surface which are represented in a Bidirectional Reflection Distribution Function (BRDF).

The BRDF describes the interaction of light rays with a surface and by that, the lighting model. Based on the material properties, parts of the energy are reflected as outgoing light rays and others are refracted within the material. The calculation may have different complexities depending on the accuracy of the BRDF. Simple lighting models are Phong [92] or Blinn-Phong [7], while more complex lighting models consider a physically correct behavior using illumination with microstructures, subsurface scattering, refraction and more.

The chosen BRDF is always a trade-off between nearly physical correctness and the real-time requirement. Modern graphics engines apply a technique very close to correct physical behavior — known as Physically Based Rendering (PBR). Akenine-Möller, Haines, and Hoffman [3] provide an excellent overview of different BRDFs used in real-time rendering. To sum it up, a Physically Based Rendering (PBR) BRDF is defined with terms of geometry shadowing, microfacet distribution, and reflection/transmission and — as all BRDFs — is based on mathematical theories. The first use in computer graphics was in 1977 by Blinn [7] and later in 1982 by Cook and Torrance [11]. Today, most engines use the Cook-Torrance shading model [11] for real-time rendering [3, 62]:

$$f_r(l, v) = \frac{F(v, h, f_0)G(v, l, h)D(h, \alpha)}{4\langle n \cdot v \rangle \langle n \cdot l \rangle} \tag{2.1}$$

with $F(v, h, f_0)$ being the Fresnel formula describing reflection and transmission, $G(v, l, h)$ being the geometry shadowing part, and $D(h, \alpha)$ for microfacet distribution. This BRDF is also used for rendering in this thesis, wherefore in the following, the three different terms are described.

The Fresnel formula — named after Augustin Jean Fresnel — describes the proportion of reflection and transmission (F) of an electromagnetic wave. Depending on the two materials irradiated by the light, the refraction is calculated. In most real-time computer graphics, one of the materials is assumed to be air or vacuum, whereby the refraction index of one material is mostly assumed to be 1. By that, the final result can be calculated more easily, although it is physically incorrect. The refraction index as well as the angles of incidence and refraction are necessary for determining this ratio. An approximation of the Fresnel formula by Christophe Schlick also assumes that one material is air [104]. Schlick [104] defined an approximation of the *Fresnel* term to render materials in realtime:

$$F(v, h, f_0) = f_0 + (1 - f_0)(1 - \langle v \cdot h \rangle)^5 \tag{2.2}$$

with f_0 as the reflection at normal angle incidence.

Perfectly smooth surfaces can rarely be found in the real world. Therefore, the geometry shadowing (G) part calculates the amount of occlusion of the material. Materials contain microscopically small unevennesses which have different effects on the refraction of the visible light. This irregularity is represented in the BRDF by the roughness of the material — the rougher the material, the higher the occlusion and as a result, the material has a more diffuse reflection. Heitz et al. [38] tested different versions of geometry shadowing calculations and suggests to use the simplest form where masking and shadowing are calculated separately:

$$G(v, l, h) = G_1(l)G_1(v) \tag{2.3}$$

Heitz et al. separate the terms into a masking and a shadowing component [38]. Based on that, Lagarde and Rousiers [62] suggest the following formula:

$$G_1(v) = \langle n \cdot v \rangle * \sqrt{(-\langle n \cdot v \rangle * \alpha^2 + \langle n \cdot v \rangle) * \langle n \cdot v \rangle + \alpha^2} \tag{2.4}$$

The third term of Equation 2.1 is the microfacet distribution (D). Different surface reflection and transmission approaches are based on the idea that surfaces (rough to smooth) can be described statistically with a collection of small microfacets. These distribution of small microfacets can be understood as many normals over the surface [114]. In a BRDF, this term is described by a Normal Distribution Function (NDF), and as with reflection and geometry, there are different approaches to compute the distribution. The best known are Oren-Nayar, Beckmann NDF and GGX NDF [3]. As an example, the GGX (Trowbridge-Reitz) approximation for NDF discovered by Walter et al. [114] and used in this thesis is defined as:

$$D(h, \alpha) = \frac{\alpha^2}{\pi((\alpha^2 - 1)\cos^2 \Phi + 1)^2} \qquad (2.5)$$

2.2 Global Illumination

Global Illumination (GI) is a collection of techniques and approaches which enable the generation of physically plausible images. Physical laws such as energy conservation, reflection, and refraction are considered. In general, GI can be divided into two procedures. The first set of methods are ray tracing approaches — often extended by photon mapping — which are mainly used in offline rendering applications. The second set of procedures is related to rasterization which is used for real-time rendering. All methods try to solve the rendering equation and thereby create photorealistic images. Depending on the application it is mostly a trade-off between performance (rasterization) and visual quality (ray tracing). Thus, the approaches in this thesis are designed for rasterization rather than ray tracing.

2.2.1 Ray Tracing

In the 19th century, Carl Friedrich Gauß pursued rays through lenses, which marks the beginning of ray tracing [91]. Nowadays, it is the basis for the propagation of the light waves sent by a light source. In computer graphics, a ray is traced based on the position and light direction until it hits a surface. At this point, the rendering equation (cf. Section 2.1) is used which predicts what happens to the energy of this ray.

All ray tracers have certain definitions in common which also apply for rasterization [91]:

Cameras The camera (sometimes called eye) is a point in 3D space the scene is viewed from. It is often described with physical quantities such as a sensor, aperture, shutter speed, and ISO. As with a real camera, the sensor has a certain resolution with $n \times m$ pixels and represents the final output. In a conventional ray tracer, light rays hitting a virtual sensor are recorded. However, backwards ray tracing is more common, in which the rays are cast from the camera's point of view.

Lightsources Light sources allow the camera to perceive objects. Each type of light source is specified by a position, direction, and intensity. In nature, light is sent from the light source, is refracted several times until it hits the retina or sensor. But as already mentioned, this is different with backwards ray tracing.

Geometry Geometries are objects in 3D space that are hit by the ray to calculate the light. Objects in computer graphics are often represented as (partially textured) triangles. In simple ray tracers, objects can also be represented as geometric shapes such as spheres or cubes. Each object in the 3D scene goes through an intersection test to find out if a ray intersects the object.

The emission and tracing of many rays need a high computation time, which has to be considered using ray tracing even nowadays. Figure 2.2 (a) shows the basic principle of a ray tracer and the basic concept of a view ray hitting a surface and checking the light. Based on this theory, different global illumination effects can be computed out-of-the-box because the physical behavior of light is simulated. Light effects like indirect lighting, caustics, or shadowing are part of the light transport as long as the materials and lights are defined correctly. Therefore path tracing — or sometimes called Monte-Carlo ray tracing — is used which is an extension to the common ray tracing [46, 54]. It allows a more advanced visualization due to randomly reflected rays from the hitting point with a surface. Figure 2.2 (b) shows a final result with different light effects and materials.

Modern graphic applications, like computer games, use ray tracing in combination with a real-time rasterization rendering. Most effects are rendered with rasterization and only special effects like indirect lighting or ambient occlusion are calculated using ray tracing. In this thesis, ray tracing is combined with rasterization to calculate reflections as part of a screen space reflection approach.

2.2.2 Rasterization

A monitor screen is assumed as a grid with many cells that may have different colors. Each cell is a display-encoded red, green and blue (RGB) triplet and the combination of the colors is the output of an application [3]. Depending on the resolution and size of the screen, the final result may consist of very fine details like in modern high-definition displays.

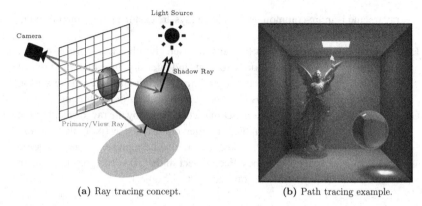

(a) Ray tracing concept.   (b) Path tracing example.

Figure 2.2 Every pixel on the camera plane emits a ray into the 3D scene depending on the position and orientation of the camera. This ray is traced inside the scene either hitting a surface or not. Depending on the surface and the lights inside the scene different effects can be calculated like indirect lighting, caustics, and shadows

Nowadays Graphical Processing Units (GPUs) are used to render complex scenes in realtime using rasterization. Even ray tracing is possible on modern desktop PC GPUs using special hardware units on the device. However, the basic idea of rasterization is conceivably simple and has proven itself in computer graphics. All approaches in this thesis also use rasterization for rendering and calculating the environment light. They rely on some basic concepts such as shader, render targets, or rendering methods.

Shader
Assuming that a virtual camera captures the scene, the image is subdivided into a grid. Every sample of a cell in a grid is called a fragment which usually represents a pixel on the screen. To render an object on the screen, a 3D model is transformed and drawn over several stages. In every stage, the input and output can be manipulated by small program units (shaders) — the complete pipeline is shown in Figure 2.3 for modern graphic APIs. The programming language OpenGL Shading Language (GLSL) as part of OpenGL, is very similar to C [3], and is mostly used for the approaches within this thesis.

Moreover, shaders are used for different aspects like generating the environment, rendering many lights, blending the image stream of the camera to the environment, perform precomputation tasks, and many more.

Figure 2.3 To transform a virtual object onto a screen, several stages are needed which are part of modern graphic APIs. Each is partly programmable with a so-called shader. Here, the pipeline is shown to compute the final output. The filled boxes cannot be manipulated by shader code

Render targets
The result from the shader is drawn on the screen, image/texture or memory. A texture for rendering output is called a fragment buffer or render target and is specified of width, height, and data format. Depending on the application, information inside a render target doesn't have to contain visual information only. As an example, a render target can be used for storing preliminary data for various graphic effects. This thesis uses render targets for fast environment lighting estimation. Moreover, render targets are used for visualization on the screen like the mixed reality output.

Rendering methods
Modern applications often use a high number of different lights and complex geometry. Therefore, deferred rendering is often used in real-time graphics reducing complexity. For this purpose, a geometry buffer (G-Buffer) stores multiple render targets containing information about the geometry of the scene from the camera's perspective [3]. The G-Buffer contains information like colors, normals, and depth values of the surfaces. Depending on the implementation, specular components, motion vectors, or masking can also be included. Deferred rendering allows for visualizing scenes with many lights as well as the calculation of different post-processing effects.

Various rendering methods utilize the G-Buffer, such as deferred rendering or tile-based deferred rendering. Newer graphics, like tiled forward rendering, do not necessarily require a G-Buffer but still often create parts of it (normal and depth) for further post processing [36, 87]. With these rendering methods, many lights can be rendered inside a scene with high performance. In this thesis, deferred rendering is used for mixed reality visualization supporting different types of light.

Global Illumination using rasterization

The idea of rasterization can also be used to enable Global Illumination (GI) effects. Computing global illumination effects using rasterization is more difficult in comparison to the ray tracing approach, for which reason many approaches consider a single-bounce indirect lighting only because of the real-time requirement. In 2005, Dachsbacher and Stamminger [16] presented an approach called Reflective Shadow Map (RSM). It extends default shadow maps including additional buffers for world positions, normal values, and the color of the surfaces. This approach provides the basis of many following rendering techniques because it offers real-time capabilities. Therefore, the additional buffers are utilized in combination with a screen-space technique achieving interactive frame rates even for complex scenes.

An extension to RSM was presented by Ritschel et al. [98] in 2008 called Imperfect Shadow Map (ISM) which creates low-resolution shadow maps and store them in an atlas. The final shadow map atlas can be used for indirect illumination in fully dynamic scenes. Another approach by Kaplanyan and Dachsbacher [51] demonstrated the possibilities of using a grid and Spherical Harmonics (SH) based on RSMs to achieve single-bounce indirect illumination with occlusion. With this technique, a computation time of a few milliseconds can be accomplished without requiring any precomputation. A widely-used technique presented by Crassin et al. [13] is Virtual Cone Tracing (VCT) which uses voxels storing the first light bounce inside a voxel volume with many mip levels. With a cone-based texture fetch, the stored lighting is used for a second bounce enabling indirect lighting. Based on a pre-filtered voxel representation of the scene (cf. Section 2.4), only a small number of sampling rays is required as they can be approximated via the cone. Kán and Kaufmann [48] combines ray tracing with common rasterization techniques and shows that real-time frame rates are feasible with multiple bounces of indirect light rays by using Monte Carlo integration on the GPU. In 2014, Lensing [65] developed the LightSkin approach that addressed GI in terms of diffuse and glossy surfaces which can be used for VR and MR applications. The main idea of this technique is based on irradiance caching [115] and radiance caching [57], which enable indirect light by interpolating so-called light caches that are distributed in model space on each model in the scene and thus delivers plausible results with high frame rates. In AR, the technique uses differential rendering to render shadows and lights [17]. Just to mention, other approaches use a Deep G-Buffer [75, 83], radiance caching combined with a radiance field chrominance [113], or stochastic decimation process [63].

GI has a major influence on the visualization of mixed reality environments. The final output and visualization highly depend on the environment, the scene setup, and the lighting. Factors like indirect lighting, ambient occlusion, or reflections are crucial for high-quality rendering. In this thesis, the concept of differential rendering [17] is used to enable high-quality output. Thus, different illumination effects can be rendered in mixed reality although the main focus is not on indirect lighting.

2.3 Mixed Reality

Mixed Reality (MR) encompasses all variants between the real and a virtual world [80]. There are four levels, such as pure reality, Augmented Reality (AR), Augmented Virtuality (AV), and virtual environment. The continuum in Figure 2.4 by Milgram et al. [80] shows the blending of the different spaces.

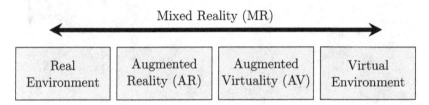

Figure 2.4 The mixed reality continuum by Milgram et al. describes any possible variant between the real environment and the virtual environment

Many people rely on Mixed Reality (MR) technologies in everyday life. More and more applications are developed inserting virtual elements in the real world to provide novel use cases. This includes simple applications like the visualization of geometric shapes on the road to simplify navigation. However, mixed reality can become rather complex as soon as objects should be imperceptible for the user. In this case, the fusion between the real and the virtual world has to be perfect.

In modern movies, it is almost impossible to distinguish between real and virtual content, but in contrast to movies, mixed reality applications have to calculate the fusion in realtime to augment the real environment with virtual objects or vise versa. This is very challenging because the surroundings are unknown, partly captured, or changing rapidly. To perform real-time augmentation of the real world by virtual content, however, five fundamental steps are necessary [19]: (1) Video recording, (2) tracking, (3) registration, (4) visualization, and (5) output. Further information is provided by Dörner et al. [19] with a detailed overview of virtual and augmented reality with further fundamentals and examples.

2.3.1 Object Detection

The detection of features offers the possibility to detect 3D points or more complex surfaces like planes or arbitrary shapes. Modern Augmented Reality (AR) Software Development Kits (SDKs) — like Google's ARCore[1] or Apple's ARKit[2] — detect such geometric shapes [8]. In Figure 2.5, detected planar surfaces by ARCore are illustrated. The small squares in the screenshot represent feature points and the different colored areas are planes detected by ARCore. Objects can then be placed on detected surfaces and accordingly registered in the real world.

Figure 2.5 3D objects can be estimated by detecting feature points inside the camera image. In this figure, a horizontal plane with some feature points (small squares) are detected. In the magnifier, the plane and the points are highlighted for better visualization

As shown in Figure 2.5, the surfaces are geometrically registered on real-world surfaces taking physical properties into account. The tracking and geometric registration results offer a first rough estimation of the existing geometry in space. In the future, the detection of real-world geometry might be almost perfect by detecting more complex geometry. But nowadays, the estimation is limited to detecting points, planes, and — depending on the SDK — simple arbitrary geometry. Modern mobile devices combine the estimation with several sensors to improve the quality. The approaches in this thesis use Google's ARCore for video recording, tracking,

---

[1] https://developers.google.com/ar/, accessed 25.03.2020
[2] https://developer.apple.com/augmented-reality/, accessed 25.03.2020

object detection, and registration. Especially the detected planes are used to place objects and to enable different light effects.

2.3.2   Light Estimation

The lighting of the environment has to be taken into account for the seamless integration of virtual elements into the real world. Ideally, a perfectly reconstructed environment exists to enable an perfect photometric registration. In this case, from any point in space the incident light on the virtual object can be calculated. Such reconstruction does not exist nowadays, because it would require a large amount of storage and the real-time requirement would be hard to solve. Apart from the environment, the detection of material and light properties is of particular difficulty. To be able to illuminate objects correctly, however, various possibilities allowing the reconstruction of the real world.

Today's industrial standard is the reconstruction of the lighting built into the AR frameworks ARKit and ARCore which offer similar lighting reconstruction features [8]. Overall, lighting reconstruction can be divided into three categories: ambient intensity, environment ambient lighting, and environment High Dynamic Range HDR lighting with reflection [8]. The ambient intensity is a value between 0 and 1 including a color-correction estimation which is analyzed by using the camera image. Furthermore, the environment ambient lighting provides a main light source with light intensity and direction. Additionally, a ambient lighting is determined using Spherical Harmonics (SH) coefficients [72], which allow diffuse illumination [95]. The environment HDR lighting allows for specular reflections. This is possible by creating a reflection cubemap that is filled with data while running the application. ARKit, for example, fills the cubemap based on detected planes while missing regions are filled with the help of artificial intelligence. ARCore uses the current camera image without additional information, also in combination with a neural network. A more detailed overview of different light reconstruction techniques are shown in Section 2.4.

Figure 2.6 shows the difference between the types of light estimations in ARCore. The first image (a) shows ambient lighting using SH. The second image (b) shows the same lighting but with an estimated main light applying shadows. And in combination with the HDR environment estimation (c), the visual quality of the virtual object is at its best. The object is a metal solid robot that looks very realistic in (c) in comparison to (a) and (b).

The light estimation of Google's ARCore is used in this thesis to estimate the main light and to apply correct shadows on the ground. Light estimations techniques like the ambient lighting and the HDR environment lighting is not used. Instead, this thesis shows approaches competing with the lighting strategies built-in the AR SDKs by a novel reconstruction of the environment.

2.4   Reconstruction

The reconstruction of the environment yields three different problems. First, it is of high relevance to analyze the geometry of the environment to take geometrical properties into account like occlusions or spatial influence between objects. Second, the structure of the surface including geometry and material has to be considered — for example, a smooth reflective surface has fundamentally different properties

(a) Ambient lighting only.   (b) Ambient lighting with shadows.

(c) HDR lighting with reflections and shadows.

Figure 2.6 Each light estimation in ARCore has different effects when rendering virtual objects. The upper row shows ambient lighting (a) with shadows in (b). The screenshot (c) use an estimated HDR environment with reflections on the surface

than a diffuse or rough surface. Third, the light of the environment is particularly important, especially enabling reflections on smooth surfaces for a plausible visualization. To enable plausible lighting and reflections, the scene has to be reconstructed for an enhanced photometric registration — which is one of the main goals of the approaches within this thesis.

The reconstruction of the environment can be done in several ways. Different approaches use different kinds of sensors to enable a proper reconstruction. In the past few years, many devices have been developed and are available for researchers and developers. However, the most common sensors are conventional cameras with fish-eye lenses, several cameras with a fixed orientation, 360-degree cameras, and depth sensors. Depending on the approach, they can be used to record and reconstruct environmental characteristics and they can capture geometry, lighting, or both information at the same time. Different drawbacks and advantages exist depending on the sensor/device wherefore the following sections describes a general overview of geometry, material and light reconstruction with related state of the art.

2.4.1 Geometry

Depth sensors are used to record the geometry of the environment efficiently. The depth data is combined with the position of the camera to calculate 3D points in space — called a point cloud. Usually, the point cloud is progressively extended and improved by continuously recording the environment. Thus, complete areas, buildings, rooms or street sections can be recorded depending on the resolution and complexity of the spatial surrounding. A high-performance sensor — such as the FARO 3D scanner — is required to record large areas with many details. Smaller environments like indoor office rooms may be captured by smaller depth sensors, stereo cameras, or by a single camera with motion information.

The storage of the real-world geometry structures can be done in several ways. A common method is to use a voxel structure filled with data from the sensors. The voxel structure is generally a 3D grid, where each data point corresponds to a geometric object [12]. Thus, a voxel always contains the information whether the geometry is present and can additionally contain information on material and light properties. Depending on the resolution of the grid, the quality of the structure is different, wherefore hierarchical structures are used to be able to represent even fine surfaces and larger areas [60]. The advantage of voxel structures is the fact that they are very easily traversable [12]. Simple cutting tests can efficiently query the data structure for geometry and light information.

The localization, mapping, and reconstruction of the spatial environment can be categorized as 2.5D depth maps approaches [77], point-based approaches [21, 55, 117], volumetric approaches [23, 39, 56, 102, 122–124], and object/mesh-based methods [93, 103, 118]. Some of these approaches are even possible on mobile devices [45, 105].

A first high quality, real-time capable dense Simultaneous Localization and Mapping (SLAM) technique, using a volumetric description was shown by Newcombe, Lovegrove, and Davison [85], which estimates depth maps which are used to create surface patches with a large number of vertices. The proposed volume is captured using a single RGB camera to estimate the depth in combination with Structure From Motion (SFM). Another important contribution was made by KinectFusion [43, 84]. Here, point clouds are obtained by a Microsoft Kinect to combine the data to a voxel volume in realtime in which points are saved in a fixed size grid with a Truncated Signed Distance Function (TSDF). This technique is a popular pipeline that has become the standard for many further SLAM techniques. Another related approach is Kintinuous [116], which keeps the camera in the center of the voxel volume and allow for a significantly larger reconstruction — data outside the volume is stored in a different manner. Another technique is voxel hashing by Nießner et al. [86] based on KinectFusion allowing a larger reconstruction size that relies on a hash table storing voxel blocks. In 2015, Kahler et al. [45] presented a SLAM pipeline based on voxel hashing that runs on mobile hardware. Voxel hashing has become a popular technique because it allows for faster voxel accesses and less memory overhead compared to tree structures. Kunert, Schwandt, and Broll [59, 60] proposes a novel technique which enables fast integration of point cloud data into a hierarchical voxel structure which allows for large-scale reconstructions at high frame rates.

Inside this thesis, a geometry estimation is utilized to estimate surfaces that are used for calculating reflections and occlusion between the real and virtual world. Moreover, a manipulation of the real world is possible by modifying the estimated data. In contrast to the state of the art, the approaches in this thesis rely on the detected objects by the AR framework rather than depth sensors. The usage of depth sensors is partly tested for the occlusion between the real and the virtual world.

2.4.2 Material

To compute realistic reflections on virtual and real-world objects, the surface needs to be analyzed to get material information which can be done with a Bidirectional Texture Function (BTF). BTF by Cula and Dana [15] is one of the most important techniques with related research by Dror, Adelson, and Willsky [20], Goldman et al. [29], and Dong et al. [18], which demonstrates the detection of specific material attributes. A major disadvantage is the performance because the attributes cannot be calculated in realtime. Meka et al. [78] introduced an advanced approach using machine learning to detect more complex materials, which is based on earlier research [79] where the reflectance and shading of surfaces can be separated in realtime. Like other material estimation approaches, it is also related to light source reconstruction.

With a material estimation, the approaches in this thesis show the effect of different light and material attributes in a MR environment. The material estimation is done manually by the user and semi-automatic by applying a default material to the ground. Previously shown research are interesting for further research.

2.4.3 Light

This thesis separates the light reconstruction into two main areas: (1) local light sources and (2) global light source.

Local Light Sources: Local light sources have an position in 3D space which can be either light bulbs, or self-emitting surfaces like a television screen — so-called area lights. Detecting light sources, as already mentioned, is related to detecting material properties. As an example, Loper and Black [70] showed an technique called differentiable rendering allowing light and material estimation based on photos. Other approaches detect local light sources by using a object with an appropriate material with known reflective information [4, 22, 35, 69]. Based on the detected reflection on the object, light sources are approximated or the incident light is calculated in certain points. In combination, it is possible to locate the light source's position, direction, and intensity. Some approaches use the current camera image and estimate light sources inside the stream and try to track them over time by using image processing [70] or neural networks [119]. Kán and Kaufmann [49] calculate the main light source depending on a single RGB-D image with a neural network.

In contrast to these research, the approaches in this thesis rely on the local light estimation provided by the ARCore SDK. As already mentioned, the SDK estimates the main light source with direction and intensity without using depth sensors while other local light sources are not taken into account.

Global Light Sources: A global light source can be understood as the light surrounding the camera and the local objects inside the scene. Usually, a 360-degree environment image is used for this purpose, which can be captured inside a light probe to store the light radiation at a certain point in the scene for further usage. Ideally, the scene consists of many light probes at every point in space to capture all light and use it for reflection rendering, but in practice, this is not feasible due to complexity, render time, and memory requirements. So, only a few light probes or even only one light probe is placed inside the scene and updated sequentially or only if necessary.

The data structure of a light probe is represented by a cubemap. Figure 2.7 (a) illustrate a cubemap with environment information which can be used for lighting. The image information in the cubemap is visualized in Low Dynamic Range (LDR) although HDR information can also be stored, which depends on the used sensors or techniques to capture the light. In Figure 2.7 (b), the cubemap is converted to a spherical (equirectangular) panorama. Both representations are used within this thesis.

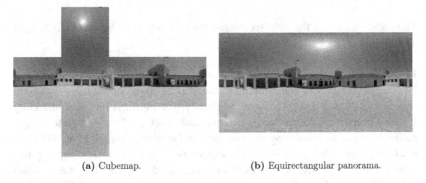

(a) Cubemap.   (b) Equirectangular panorama.

Figure 2.7 The cubemap is divided into six faces for every single orientation. Each side of a cubemap may be used for storing the illumination of the environment. So, any reflection of a surface can be used to fetch texel data from the cubemap. This example shows a captured environment as a unfolded cubemap (a) and a spherical (equirectangular) panorama (b)

The visualization of light with a cubemap is called environment illumination which can be done, as already mentioned, using hardware or even software approaches. In this thesis, the focus is on software-based techniques without the use of additional hardware. Nevertheless, an overview of the different state of the art is described in the following. All of the approaches have in common that they capture the lighting of the environment to show diffuse and/or glossy reflection on virtual objects.

Generating proper glossy reflections can be done in several ways, e.g. by capturing real-world objects. As an example, State et al. [111] and Debevec [17] have used a mirroring ball (glass or chrome ball) placed inside the real-world scene, which allows the usage of the reflected information of the ball as background illumination information. Then, a light probe is generated, by combining the reflected information of the ball and the camera image. During capturing, HDR is used in combination with a differential renderer to achieve higher quality. This technique requires preparation of the scene and the presence and tracking of the mirroring object, making it unsuitable for everyday applications.

Other approaches [32, 96, 100] rely on different camera techniques like multiple cameras or special lenses. In 2007, Grosch, Eble, and Mueller [32] captured the lighting inside a one-side-opened box by capturing the illumination outside the scene with a HDR fish-eye camera to simulate indirect lighting. The drawback is the preparation using the camera with the fish-eye lens. Another technique — known as Delta Voxel Cone Tracing (DVCT) — by Franke [24] is based on the earlier mentioned VCT [13]. The result performs in interactive frame rates with diffuse, glossy, and specular indirect reflections between real and virtual surfaces. Franke [24] also captured light conditions based on a fish-eye camera and allows real-time glossy inter-reflections between real and virtual objects. Multiple cameras with fish-eye lenses can also be used to capture ambient illumination, like Rohmer et al. [100], who used a stationary PC, a tracking system, and multiple cameras for computing environment lighting. The captured light information of any camera is combined to generate the lighting information, which enables highly realistic virtual reflections in realtime on mobile devices. Using multiple cameras or special hardware is a common way to capture environment illumination because it offers the possibility to capture the ambient lighting in realtime. However, the usage of multiple cameras, fish-eye lenses, objects with a reflecting material, and even a stationary tracking system is not applicable for most MR applications in daily life.

To capture the environment, a more applicable way is the usage of the camera image only like the approach by Karsch et al. [53] which analyze the scene and search for a comparable environment map from a digital library. Glossy reflections are supported but could be misleading because the environment maps do not necessarily provide accurate information whereby especially objects with a flat mirror-like surface may not be displayed correctly. Moreover, depending on the size of the digital library, no image might be available that is close to ground truth.

Some current mobile devices have a depth camera (RGB-D camera), in addition to the default color camera, which can also be used for global environment estimation. Gruber, Richter-Trummer, and Schmalstieg [33] and Gruber, Ventura, and Schmalstieg [34] showed an approach for real-time GI using a depth sensor which estimates general diffuse lighting based on a 3D reconstruction of the scene together with SH. Richter-Trummer et al. [97] presented an technique for recovering incident lighting with a surface material reconstruction. The scene is scanned by an RGB-D sensor to segment different objects and materials and by solving the inverse rendering problem. So, it can be used for lighting a scene even with new light properties. Mirror-like reflections are not supported because the light estimation supports diffuse lighting only which is a drawback of this approach. In general, depth sensors have a limited detection range, which implies that spacious surroundings like outdoor environments cannot be easily recorded. For this reason, depth sensors for lighting reconstruction are not used in this thesis.

Ropinski, Wachenfeld, and Hinrichs [101] presented an approach for creating a light probe every frame using an image stream without a depth sensor at which each virtual object inside the scene is handled separately and generate multiple cubemaps. Each cubemap is used for calculating the reflection of the objects, whereby the performance heavily depends on the number of virtual objects inside the scene, especially as soon as the information has to be updated frequently. Kán, Unterguggenberger, and Kaufmann [50] showed the generation of a 360-degree environment map by scanning the environment before visualizing virtual objects. Depending on the environment, the result is filtered according to different material types and the illumination is estimated, which is not practical for altering lighting conditions and moving objects. Another possibility for single image lighting estimation is image stitching to create a 360-degree panorama. In general, such techniques are subdivided in camera-based [1, 10, 68, 74], feature-based [6, 81, 94], and photogrammetry-based approaches. Most of these approaches use multiple images with overlapping image information [47, 112]. Liao et al. [68] presented an approach for spherical panorama image stitching in which the position of the camera has to be static or manually adjusted by the user. Chew and Lian [10] presented a panorama stitching system using only one single camera based on the overlapping of two adjacent images. The technique uses Speeded Up Robust Features (SURF) to detect features between two images and stitch them together based on a weighted projection while the real-time stitching of the adjacent images was not addressed. Following the approach by Ropinski, Wachenfeld, and Hinrichs [101], in this thesis the implementation of 360-degree lighting is used by estimating a single global light probe that can be used for several objects at the same time. Further, a stitching technique based on Liao et al. [68] is used for environment lighting estimation, which is extended by a free camera movement and solves the problem of uncaptured parts.

In contrast to a sequence of camera images, several approaches exist which reconstruct the environment based on a single image using a neural network for the task of reconstructing the ambient lighting [41, 78, 88, 110, 121]. In 2017, Mandl et al. [73] showed the usage of a Convolution Neural Network (CNN) to estimate a highly accurate result which can be used for photorealistic rendering. Mandl et al. [73] trained the neural network with pre-illuminated models and different SH variations which are stored in a database. Depending on the current camera pose, a similar lighting from the database is used, whereby different light conditions as well as glossy reflections are not supported. Gardner et al. [26] estimates the environment using a deep neural network to estimate an indoor HDR environment and predict light sources with intensities inside a scene from a single photo. The diffuse reflection looks plausible while glossy reflections are not feasible. Based on this research, Gardner et al. [25] shows an estimation based on spatial location rather than global lighting, which offers a better visualization but only allows for diffuse reflections or illumination of rough materials. Other approaches like Georgoulis et al. [27, 28], Meka et al. [78], and Park et al. [88], estimate HDR illumination from a single image using a neural network with an reference object inside the camera view which is, as already mentioned, not applicable in everyday life. In 2019, Kán and Kaufmann [49] used a neural network to estimate the main light source depending on a single RGB-D image. Depending on the main light, the complete 360-degree environment is estimated using the technique by Gardner et al. [26], which is also not capable of estimating light probes usable for high-quality glossy reflections. Another approach by LeGendre et al. [64] captured three real-world spheres with different materials in a fixed distance to the mobile camera. This data is used to train a neural network and to estimate the indoor and outdoor environment without reference objects. Visual results show plausible reflections in different scenarios although detailed glossy reflections are not possible. The general technique by LeGendre et al. [64] is included in the ARCore SDK since version 1.10 for the HDR cubemap API.

The previously introduced research can be used for global light reconstruction to estimate the ambient lighting. Table 2.3 summarize a selection of these approaches to give an overview of the differences. The selection was made depending on the techniques and the requirements.

2.5   Neural Networks & Deep Learning

The approaches in this thesis partly use deep learning to predict the environment. Therefore, some basic concepts and terminologies are described in the following. Goodfellow, Bengio, and Courville [30] offer a detailed overview of neural networks and deep learning for further reading.

Neural networks must be appropriately trained with data — the so-called training or learning phase. There are three types of training/learning:

Unsupervised Learning — or unlabeled learning — is the learning of categories based on a lot of data. The neural network has no information on the meaning of the data but can categorize the data later. This is often used to form groups/categories or to make forecasts on a dataset. [2, 82]

Reinforcement Learning is similar to unsupervised learning. However, in this case, the neural network is told the quality of the prediction. The information about the quality is calculated and returned to the network. A possible application might be a neural network that learns to play computer games. As an example, the network is predefined with the rules of the game. In every step the quality of the current move is calculated depending on the score. [2, 30]

Supervised Learning — or labeled learning — are data with annotations regarding a context. In practice, this is often related to a image with a specific content like cats or dogs. Thus, a neural network can learn to distinguish between different content and categories. [2, 82]

A neural net is trained on a learning data set, which mostly consist of about 80% to 90% of the entire data (learning). The rest (10% to 20%) will be used for validation in a later step [30]. Neural network data sets often consist of several thousand to millions of data points, which are used to train the neural network across several epochs. After an epoch every data has been seen at least once and the result is tested with the validation data set. The result of the validation is compared to the result of the neural network to provide information about the quality of the neural network. According to Goodfellow, Bengio, and Courville [30], the optimal capacity of data is reached as soon as the training error is low and the generalization error slightly increase.

Inside the neural network, the data is manipulated and analyzed multiple times — step-by-step or layer-by-layer until it reaches a output layer [82]. In addition to the possibility to use many layers, layers can also be fanned out wide. However, each layer is finally connected to the successors. A neural network always consists of an input layer and an output layer with multiple hidden layers in between — the more layers a network has, the deeper it is.

Each layer consists of a defined number of units — often called neurons — while each unit in a layer is linked to the previous and the following layer. Between each connection of the units, a weight is used which represents the information of a neural network. These weights can change over time to improve the quality of the neural network by adjusting them in each layer after every cycle, depending on the output

Table 2.3 Summary of different approaches estimating environment lighting

Year	Author	Input	Technique / requirements
1998	Debevec [17]	RGB	Real-world reference object / mirroring ball in the scene
2004	Ropinski, Wachenfeld, and Hinrichs [101]	RGB	Creation of multiple environment cubemaps using single camera image
2007	Grosch, Eble, and Mueller [32]	RGB	Fish-eye lens capturing the daylight from outside
2011	Liao et al. [68]	RGB	Image stitching using multiple images with a fixed camera position
2014	Franke [24]	RGB-D	Depth camera and fish-eye lens
2014	Rohmer et al. [100]	RGB	Multiple cameras inside the real world to capture all incident lighting
2014	Karsch et al. [53]	RGB	Static digital library with multiple environment maps
2017	Georgoulis et al. [27]	RGB	Real-world reference material inside the scene analyzed by a neural network
2017	Mandl et al. [73]	RGB	Neural network trained with a 3D model to illuminate the same in the real world
2017	Gardner et al. [26]	RGB	Indoor environment and light source estimation based on a single image using a neural network
2019	Káan and Kaufmann [49]	RGB-D	Environment estimation based on depth camera and main light estimation with neural network
2019	LeGendre et al. [64]	RGB	Record of three reference spheres with a mobile camera to train a neural network

quality. Based on the weights, an activation function calculates if the data will be transmitted to the next unit. Therefore, different activation functions can be used for several architectures [2, 30, 82].

A neural network architecture, used in this thesis, is the Generative Adversarial Network (GAN). The applications of GANs are mostly the generation of photo-realistic images, the creation of 3D models, the extraction of 3D objects from 2D images, or the creation of music. GANa consists of two artificial neural networks working against each other [2, 14, 31]. A generator produces results based on the given network architecture and input/training data. Finally, the generator is capable to learn plausible results based on the training. A discriminator, as the second network, is trained to judge the results of the generator by estimating if the input is real or fake. Thus, the generator tries to produce progressively better results and the output should gradually become more plausible over time. In this thesis, the GAN architecture by Pathak et al. [89] is the basis for semantic inpainting to estimate the environment lighting on top of the stitching approach.

Illumination in Mixed Reality

3

Illumination is important for a high-quality visualization of virtual objects. Especially in the case of AR applications, lighting is important to visualize virtual objects inside the real world correctly. A major contribution to AR lighting is the reflection of the real environment on virtual objects. Therefore, the environment needs to be taken into account for proper rendering.

The illumination of virtual objects in AR environments is of particular importance if a high degree of realism has to be achieved. To visualize the lighting, various information are necessary, such as material and lighting properties of the virtual and real world. In this way, various mutual influences such as reflections on the object can be rendered. Without these reflections, only simple materials such as rough plastic surfaces can be represented rather than surfaces such as shinny metals. To enable plausible and realistic lighting, this thesis examines the lighting in MR using conventional hardware. The first step is the scene reconstruction (cf. Section 3.1), which enables mutual influences between the virtual and real world. In particular, the focus is on the reconstruction of the spatial information, the materials, and local light sources. The spatial information is mostly used for occlusion or shadows. Materials provide information about the nature of a surface and thus enable different lighting effects. The lighting is made possible by various light sources such as the main light which can be reconstructed using an AR/MR framework. Another important light source is the environment light, which is determined in the second step (cf. Section 3.2). The determination of the environment light is the core of this thesis, which is divided into four different approaches. All four approaches

Electronic supplementary material The online version of this chapter (https://doi.org/10.1007/978-3-658-35192-2_3) contains supplementary material, which is available to authorized users.

T. Schwandt, *High-Quality Illumination of Virtual Objects Based on an Environment Estimation in Mixed Reality Applications*,
https://doi.org/10.1007/978-3-658-35192-2_3

have in common that they create a 360-degree lighting of the environment without additional hardware. For this purpose, the current camera image is transformed, combined with past information, and semantically inpainted by a neural network. The last step for lighting in mixed reality is to apply the environment map to the virtual objects (cf. Section 3.3). For this, light probes are used which are filtered to correspond with the physically-based rendering. A suitable filtering is required since it is a performance-intensive process which has to be computed on mobile devices. By filtering the environment lighting in combination with the scene reconstruction, high-quality reflections between the virtual and real world can be rendered. This whole concept of lighting reconstruction is considered in more detail in this chapter.

3.1   Scene Reconstruction

In recent years, researchers explored several approaches to capture different aspects of the environment. This information is used in different purposes like indoor navigation, mapping of objects, or tracking objects inside the scene. Especially, spatial information needs to be reconstructed and stored for further processing and for a realistic integration of virtual objects inside the real environment. As soon as physical interactions between virtual objects and the real world should exist, the scene has to be analyzed. Such interaction can be physical behavior, occlusion, or any kind of visual dependency. In the following, the scene reconstruction is examined for spatial information, materials, and local light sources.

3.1.1   Spatial Information

The capturing of spatial information is needed to calculate physical behaviors between real and virtual objects as well as occlusion or visual interactions. Especially visual interactions are important in the case of highly-realistic visualization. For example, mirror-like reflections between virtual objects and the real environment are only possible with sufficient information of the real world.

Existing approaches reconstruct as much 3D information of the real environment as possible by using several kinds of sensors such as RGB-D cameras, which allow the reconstruction of spatial information by combining the depth and the color of both information. Other approaches use different hardware for scanning the environment, such as laser scanners or stereo cameras. Modern mobile devices use integrated sensors (GPS, gyro-sensors, front- and back-facing cameras, and sometimes even depth sensors) for spatial reconstruction. If no depth sensors exist, other approaches like stereo matching or depth from motion (sometimes using neural networks) can be used — a more detailed review can be found in Section 2.4.1.

The approaches in this thesis use a conventional camera in a mobile device (smartphone) to determine the spatial environment. For this purpose, object recognition in the AR framework ARCore is used mostly. However, since ARCore only allows for simple geometric shapes like planes, a depth sensor has been tested to determine more detailed information about objects in space. The goal is to allow occlusion, for example, of one's own hand in the MR environment. Therefore, the information of the real environment like the geometry and materials are transferred to the virtual world.

In this thesis, a depth map in combination with color data is used to estimate real-world geometry and transfer it into a data storage. Thus, based on the depth image, a normal map can to be calculated. Generally, quite a number of techniques exist to estimate a normal map from a depth image, like the approach by Lensing and Broll [67], who shows the generation of a normal map in each frame with some improvements in the reconstruction step. Based on this approach and the acquired depth image, the normal information is calculated and directly stored inside the G-Buffer. The generation of normal maps from raw depth data input often leads to insufficient quality [67] because it depends on the sensor and the used algorithm. Some problems are varying depth values, temporal incoherence, and insufficient depth resolution. Lensing and Broll [67] provide a filtering technique to solve some of these problems. The filtering technique is Guided Image Filter (GIF) to filter the depth image and calculate more accurate normal maps. This approach is the base for further exploration.

Using GIF shows to be a sufficient image filter with some limitations like: varying depth values from frame to frame, regions without depth information, insufficient lateral resolution, and uneven normal maps. Therefore, a new pipeline is suggested with the following steps [106]:

1. Map the depth image to the color space
2. Crop the center part if necessary (depth and color)
3. Apply an inpainting to the depth image to fill missing regions
4. Use GIF to smooth the depth without losing edges
5. Build normal map by blending an estimated scene geometry

Mapping, cropping, and inpainting: Depending on the sensor, different SDKs are provided which offers the possibility to map the color space to the depth space or vise versa. This mapping is necessary because a small physical offset exists between the depth and the color camera. Figure 3.1 shows a color image of the Microsoft

Kinect V2 (a) and a mapped depth image in (b). Figure Inside the depth image, it is clearly visible that the outer areas of the color image is not captured and some depth shadowing exists (rectangle).

(a) Color image.   (b) Mapped depth to color.

Figure 3.1 The information of the depth stream can be mapped to the color space. Some unknown areas at the border and depth shadowing happen because of different image resolution and distances between the sensors

After the mapping, a cropping is applied to both images. Especially the color frame needs to be cropped because the resolution of the depth image is lower than the color image when using the Microsoft Kinect V2. Remaining holes inside the depth images can be filled using inpainting — an approach that had not been investigated in this thesis.

Filtering: A noisy depth image like in Figure 3.1 does not allow for directly storing depth and normal data in the G-Buffer since the depth and normal data would be insufficient for further rendering. Before storing the depth data in the G-Buffer, GIF [37] is applied, which creates smoother depth values without losing edge information at the same time. Filters like a bilateral blur are also common to enhance the quality of the depth image but the base approach by Lensing and Broll [67] showed that GIF produces reliable results when applied to the depth image.

Creating and blending the normal map: Based on the filtered depth image the normal map is calculated which can be done by using different techniques. A possible approach would be to create normal maps by checking the surrounding depth values and calculating a normal from those values. Though, this reconstruction of normals leads to continuously changing normals frame by frame because of temporal incoherence in the depth image. To overcome this issue, a blending with an approximated geometry is applied to the constantly changing normal values before adding them to the G-Buffer. This approximated geometry can be a plane but also any other 3D object. In this case, the simple geometry detection by ARCore or any other AR framework can be used. However, depending on the angle between the geometry normal and the normal of the depth image both values are blended in which the dot product of both normals is used as the weighting factor. During testing, several blending functions like Reoriented Normal Mapping (RNM) have been tested as well as the result without blending. Thereby, the blending with an angle-related weighting shows to be the most promising approach.

Figure 3.2 illustrates the effectiveness of blending with the angle between both normals. As already mentioned, the approximated geometry may be a plane or any other low polygon model. In the case of Figure 3.2 a plane has been used. Tests indicates that blending the normal values generally leads to a better approximation of the geometry information. The variance / error value in the bottom part of the figure is lower in (b) than in (a) because the normals are more precise.

Usage: With the depth information, a more advanced visualization can be rendered. In Figure 3.3, the real environment is captured using a depth sensor — the hand is captured and the depth data can be used for occlusion. Finally, virtual objects can be integrated more realistically and allowing occlusion.

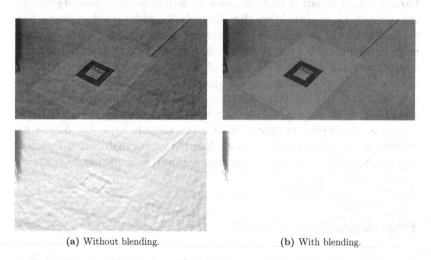

(a) Without blending.   (b) With blending.

Figure 3.2 On the left side (a) the original uneven normals without blending are shown [66]. The right side (b) shows normals blended with a plane. Both related depth maps are filtered with GIF. (Original image by Schwandt and Broll [106])

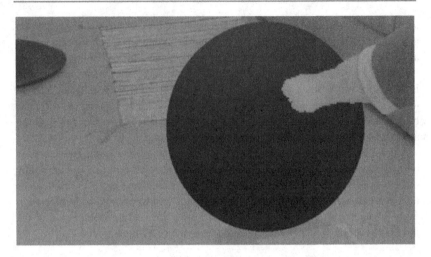

Figure 3.3 The hand is inside the virtual ball while the rest of the arm is in front of the object. This effect is possible by using a depth sensor and the depth data for occlusion estimation between the real and virtual world

Further enhancement: If no depth sensor is available, the approximated geometry can also be used. This would not allow for occlusion with complex geometry like the hand but it can be useful for simpler visual interactions. A possible situation might be a virtual object that is behind a desk which could be approximated with a small number of vertices. Even simple planes like those detected by today's AR frameworks could be used to enhance visualization. With these detected planes, depth data is more reliable and so normal estimation is better. Moreover, the detected surfaces of the framework could be sufficient for a realistic rendering too. In the near future, the depth data of an RGB-D sensor might be neglected to allow for appropriate real-time depth reconstruction based on a single RGB camera. However, reconstructing spatial information with depth sensors is more efficient than software approaches nowadays.

3.1.2   Materials

The reconstruction of material information like roughness, surface color, or metalness is a challenging and complex research task. Most research approaches (cf. Section 2.4.2) are either not usable in realtime or not reliable enough for dynamic

MR environments. The real and virtual world can only be mixed through a suitable definition of the materials. Material properties influence the lighting of the virtual and real objects, which means that the properties of both worlds must be known. Since the materials are known in the virtual world, only a material estimation of the real world is required. Section 2.4 encompasses the importance of reconstructing light and materials for realistic visualization.

In this thesis, no automatic detection of the materials is supported and no base approach is used. Instead, a previously defined material or more complex objects with different material information are placed on the ground semi-automatically or manually in 3D space. This straightforward definition of material objects is then linked to the camera image and allows quick and efficient storage in the G-Buffer. Accordingly, the color part of the material is defined by the color image, while further information is predefined by the user. Moreover, depth information is stored to enable spatial reconstruction. To overcome the issue of varying depth data from the depth sensor, the estimated planes from the ARCore SDK are used instead. Tests with a depth sensor produce unusable normal and depth data because of varying depth values. In contrast, the reconstruction of the planes provides continuous normal data which enables a more harmonious calculation of the lighting. Besides, for most AR scenarios, estimated planes are sufficient — especially if no complex reconstruction is needed.

Finally, the approach to material reconstruction is a semi-automatic placement of predefined material information in combination with the camera data for storing the color and depth data. In general, the material information is a combination of metalness, reflectance, roughness (or smoothness), and a base color — the default properties of a PBR material in a HDR pipeline. In Table 3.1, the definition of a material with the corresponding format is shown.

The default material does not have any reflection properties. As soon as special reflection behaviors should exist, the material has to be defined manually but could be detected automatically with other related approaches (cf. Section 2.4.2). However, the overall pipeline is shown in Figure 3.4 and demonstrates how material, geometry, and the image stream is stored in the G-Buffer. After the G-Buffer pass, the lighting pass unpacks the G-Buffer and uses it for different lighting effects. Finally, a mixed reality result can be shown on desktop PCs and mobile devices.

Traditionally, a G-Buffer provides information about the color and normal of each object inside the scene and the distance (depth) to the camera. Depending on the graphics engine, some extra information may be stored like normal, roughness, metallness and more (Table 3.1) [9, 52, 62]. These information are estimated and stored in the G-Buffer including all the information of the geometry and material visible by the current camera. Figure 3.5 provides an overview regarding the structure

Table 3.1 Definition of a material

Type	Format	Can have a texture?
Base color	RGB	Yes
Normal	RGB	Yes
Displacement	R	Yes
Roughness	R	Yes
Reflectance	R	No
Metallness	R	Yes
Tiling	RG	No
Offset	RG	No

of the information in the G-Buffer. In general, the G-Buffer is holding information of: normal, roughness, albedo color, reflectance $f0$, Ambient Occlusion (AO) of the object, and an material ID that can be used to distinguish between reconstructed and virtual objects.

The screen space color of the image stream is used as the albedo color of the real-world material and is multiplied with the predefined color of the virtual material. Reflectance color $f0$ is the reflected color depending on the metalness of the object and is not defined by the material. Equation 3.1 shows the calculation of the reflectance term $f0$ with R as reflectance value, M as metalness and C as base color of the material. Although some material definitions provide the information, the reflectance and albedo color can be computed by considering the base color and the metalness of the objects [62]. Equation 3.2 shows the calculation of the albedo value A.

$$f0 = 0.16 * R^2 * (1 - M) + C * M \tag{3.1}$$

$$A = C * (1 - M) \tag{3.2}$$

By placing material objects in the environment, various effects can be rendered like a manipulation of the real world by using alternative values for the spatial environment. For example, normals can be changed or the roughness does not match to the corresponding real object. Accordingly, alternative data is used when illuminating the objects which leads to a manipulated output. At the same time, with the correct definition of material and geometry, different lighting properties can be generated, such as the proportion of glossy reflections.

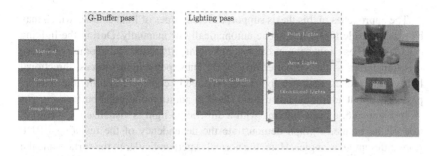

Figure 3.4 Material, geometry, and image stream are combined and packed inside the G-Buffer. Later, the G-Buffer is unpacked and every light uses the information to do the lighting. (Original image by Schwandt and Broll [107])

	R	G	B	A
G-Buffer 1	Packed Normal		Roughness	0.0
G-Buffer 2	Albedo Color			Material ID
G-Buffer 3	$f0$			AO

Figure 3.5 The G-Buffer is based on the structure from the Frostbite engine [62]. Parts of the buffer are defined via the material information like metalness and reflectance and other parts can be precalculated at runtime like $f0$. The roughness/smoothness is saved for further calculations

3.1.3 Local Light Sources

Local light sources have a major influence on the virtual and real environment. For example, light sources provide the overall visual impression as well as the existence of shadows. In mixed realities, real light sources may have an influence on the real as well as the virtual environment. The same also applies to virtual light sources, which can also influence the real environment. Thus, virtual light sources should be a good approximation of the real-world light sources to enable a high-quality and realistic visualization. In this thesis, a main light is used which is defined as a directional light with an intensity and a direction. Both values (intensity and direction) are estimated using an AR SDK. According to the estimation by the SDK, the main light source might be updated and shadows look more plausible.

The approaches in this thesis support different types of light sources which may be placed inside the virtual scene automatically or manually. During the lighting calculation, these light sources can be applied directly to the real geometry because it is transferred to the virtual environment. Thus, point light sources, directional lights, light probes, and area lights can be directly considered during the lighting pass — without additional calculation steps, or additional lighting buffers.

In Figure 3.6, a basic lighting with a directional light is visualized. On the left side of the image, a graph demonstrate the dependency of the resulting BRDF from different view angles. Here, the normal is perpendicular to the surface and the light vector is 45-degree. Material values are: roughness 0.4, reflectance 0.6, and metalness 0.0. On the right side is an example object in a real environment with the same material values. It shows a virtual head with a non-metal/plastic material inside a AR application.

By using the estimated local light source, virtual objects can be more realistically embedded in the real environment and the calculation of realistic shadows are possible. At the same time, the material estimation from Section 3.1.2 allows virtual local light sources to be embedded with an influence to the real world which also has a high impact on the visualization in mixed reality.

3.2   Environment Light

The environment light is a special light inside the scene, which is different from point light sources or area lights. Sometimes, graphics engines refer to it as a global light source or reflection probe. In fully virtual environments, the information is mostly represented as a sky with sun and clouds but it could also include other information like buildings or mountains. However, the diffuse and specular lighting of a virtual

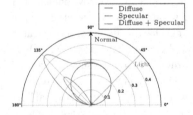

Figure 3.6 Inside this scene a directional light is visualized. A graph shows the result of the BRDF with changing view angle over the hemisphere on the left side. Based on this settings, the final result of a virtual head with a shadow on the ground is shown on the right side

object highly depends on information of the ambient lighting. Inside a complete virtual scenario, it is easy to calculate this information, but in MR, it is difficult to estimate the global environment lighting, especially if no special hardware should be used. Previous approaches often use specific techniques such as fish-eye lenses or the placement of reflecting spheres in the scene (cf. Section 2.4.3). However, this thesis provides different novel approaches to estimate the environment lighting using the camera image only.

This following section describe the approaches without using special hardware. Generally, the major goal is to estimate an environment to use it for the generation of a light probe. This light probe is used for Image-Based Lighting (IBL) enabling reflections of the incident light from a certain point in space. First, an estimation of the environment using a single image is shown. Second, a Lookup Texture (LUT) is introduced based on the single image approach to improve the overall performance significantly. Third, the estimation is further improved by a stitching approach. Lastly, the usage of a neural network in combination with the stitching approach is described.

3.2.1   Single Image Estimation

Using a single camera image for environment light estimation is not possible in case of photorealistic and physically correct images. The approach by Ropinski, Wachenfeld, and Hinrichs [101] describes the generation of environment maps from a single image by estimating the ambient light for every single virtual object in the scene whereby, as soon as the scene exceeds a certain number of virtual objects, performance issues may arise. Still, the main idea of the approach is interesting, and therefore, this thesis address the performance issue by creating a single global environment map used by all virtual objects at the same time [106]. Moreover, a light probe is computed which allows the calculation of the diffuse and glossy term in the BRDF depending on individual material properties.

A light probe contains ambient light information that is available from any point in space with the assumption that it includes the entire scene. So, the lighting at a certain point can easily be fetched from the light probe (cubemap) by simply using the normal vector of the surface which indicate the direction of the incident light. However, inside a dynamic environment — like in a MR application — the light probe is updated every frame to enable dynamic reflections. The main goal is to achieve a plausible environment map for ambient lighting reconstruction, even if it may not be physically correct. Thus, in this approach, the light probe is calculated using the current camera image by proposing an estimation where the environment map is generated by the following steps [106]:

1. Copying and flipping the image: First the image of the image stream (webcam, mobile phone, ...) is captured, copied, and flipped horizontally. The flipped image is an estimation used for the unknown environment behind the camera. In most cases the visual results are still plausible although this method produces a incorrect cubemap.

2. Segmenting images: The next step is to segment the image into the different sides of the cubemap which consists of six individual faces, one for each cardinal direction, including environment and floor.

As a start, the original and flipped image stream from the previous step is segmented into five regions which contribute to individual sides of the cubemap. Figure 3.7 shows the segmentation of the front image highlighting the contribution to the front, left, right, bottom, and top face. The back image — or flipped front image — contributes to the same faces like the front image (left, right, bottom, and top face) but to the back part instead of the front part. A part of the image stream I is extracted depending on the resolution of the cubemap O (cf. Equation 3.3). The remaining pixels of the image are then used for the side information by using a warp perspective transformation.

$$f = 1 - \frac{(min(I_{Height}, I_{Width}) - min(O_{Height}, O_{Width}))/2}{min(I_{Height}, I_{Width})} \qquad (3.3)$$

3. Combining faces: The last step is to combine the sides of the front and back image with an un-captured space between the front and back image depending on the field of view of the camera — the larger the field of view is, the smaller is this area. A 180-degree field of view would result in a complete cubemap without borders — but this is not the case with common mobile phones. Therefore, filling this space between the faces was tested by applying image inpainting, but the processing time was too long which requires further optimization similar to Herling and Broll [40]. It is important to note that the approach without inpainting also calculates a plausible quality for a light probe and a first basic assumption of the environment map. Figure 3.8 shows the combination from the segmentation to the final panorama without inpainting.

Figure 3.7 Segmentation of the image stream into five faces of a cubemap. The center part is fixed and fills the front or back part respectively. Each side information is transformed to the half of a cube side. In combination with the flipped back part, a whole cube can be estimated

Figure 3.8 The panorama is estimated by using a single input image only. In this case, the image from the segmentation is used to generate the final panorama. As a first approximation, the result shows a plausible reflection on mirror-like surfaces

3.2.2 Lookup Texture

The main problem of the described single image estimation is performance especially when inpainting is applied, FPSs are not interactive on mobile devices. Moreover, the perspective warp is also limiting the FPS significantly. So, an improvement to the previous approach is needed, which is the usage of a LUT, to execute heavy calculations in a precomputation step [109].

To sum up the single image estimation, the following steps need to be applied: (1) use a square part (variably adjustable) for the background lighting from the center of the image. The same extracted image is (2) used for the foreground illumination — applying a horizontal flip of the image. Next, the side information of the cubemap are (3) extracted from the remaining part.

As mentioned earlier, the inpainting to calculate missing side information is unnecessary for the plausibility. So the inpainting can be neglected which also results in a better performance. This means that the ambient lighting approximation is not context dependent. Therefore, the calculation can be performed to a preprocessing step. Thus, the rather complex perspective warp calculation to estimate the sides of a cubemap has to be carried out only once. Therefore, a LUT can be used consisting of homogeneous texture coordinates. This LUT is generated consisting of texture coordinates (UV coordinates) which are calculated as described in the previous approach. But in contrast to the previous approach, each UV-coordinate inside the current image stream is now related to a pixel inside the cubemap. Through this, the same visual quality can be provided but with a performance of less than a few milliseconds (cf. Section 5.3). In Figure 3.9 the LUT with a visual output is shown.

(a) LUT.   (b) Final output.

Figure 3.9 On the left side (a), the LUT is shown with homogeneous texture coordinates. Every pixel is representing a point in screen space of the current camera image. Hereby, the final result on the right side (b) are simply two texture lookups

3.2.3   Stitching

To overcome the issue of non-physical and partly non-plausible reflections, a new technique is required. This next approach should be plausible and keep the physical conditions of the real world. Moreover, additional devices such as depth sensors or fish-eye lenses should still be not part of the approach to ensure flexibility. In the following, such an approach is presented that uses only an RGB image stream for reconstructing the environment light.

As already mentioned, the approximation of the lighting behind the camera is unrealistic using the LUT because it is not based on any real information about the background. Reflections are unrealistic but plausible in most cases, but only as long as the objects have no flat surface directed towards the camera. These objects appear as if they were transparent as soon as a certain angle of reflection and particular values for smoothness and metalness of the material are given. In Figure 3.10, the problem is demonstrated inside the reflection of the hallway in the virtual head. The idea is to use a stitching approach to overcome this issue [109].

Figure 3.10 With the LUT approach, the reflection looks plausible but with some drawbacks especially on smooth materials. In this case, the reflection of the backside of the virtual head shows the door and orange reflection from the side

The stitching approach of this thesis is based on camera-based techniques like Mann and Picard [74] and Liao et al. [68]. Basically, the information of every frame from the image stream is stitched into the partly reconstructed environment information. To stitch the information correctly, the camera parameters (position, rotation, FoV, ...) are applied. This ensures that the current image stream is combined with the previous images in the right place. Thus, a more realistic and even physically plausible environment illumination is created — the more complete the stitching, the better the rendered result. Compared to Mann and Picard [74] and Liao et al. [68], this approach focuses on real-time capability and use in MR scenarios. However, it is often unlikely to get a completely stitched cubemap because users might not move around to capture the whole environment in a MR application. This issue is addressed later in Section 3.2.4.

The stitching approach, however, also highly dependent on external factors, such as the used tracking approach or the FoV of the camera. Especially when using marker-based tracking with a marker on a table, certain parts of the ceiling are never visible because the camera always has to be directed towards the marker but with feature-based approaches like ARCore, this is less of a problem. Nevertheless, if not enough feature points have been found, the issue of an incomplete cubemap persists.

Different approaches for stitching images onto the cubemap have been evaluated. First, the camera plane of the image stream is used as a physically-based assumption. Second, a non physically-based geometry has been tested like a curved plane. Both techniques make use of the geometric information, which is used to stitch the current camera image onto the cubemap.

Camera Plane

Assuming that the surrounding and the objects inside are rather far away from the camera, the use of the camera plane is a possible solution for stitching — although the assumption is not correct since some objects like tables, walls or other objects are closer to the camera. However, the far plane of the camera is tested for stitching which is extracted from the view projections matrix in each frame in combination with the current camera stream. It is assumed to be a sufficient basis for stitching because the view projection matrix follows the intrinsic and extrinsic camera parameters and is, therefore, closer to a physically-related approach.

As already mentioned, based on the extrinsic and intrinsic camera parameters and the corresponding view projection matrix, the camera parameters of the far plane and, respectively, the homogeneous UV-coordinates can be calculated. Equation 3.4 shows a generic 4×4 matrix which, in this case, is equal to a model view projection matrix.

$$MP = \begin{bmatrix} a_1 & a_2 & a_3 & a_4 \\ b_1 & b_2 & b_3 & b_4 \\ c_1 & c_2 & c_3 & c_4 \\ d_1 & d_2 & d_3 & d_4 \end{bmatrix} \tag{3.4}$$

The planes are expressed in their implicit form $Ax + By + Cz + D = 0$. Equation 3.5 shows the extraction of the far clipping plane.

$$\begin{aligned} A &= -a_3 + -a_4 \\ B &= -b_3 + -b_4 \\ C &= -c_3 + -c_4 \\ D &= -d_3 + -d_4 \end{aligned} \tag{3.5}$$

Hereby, each frustum plane is extracted from the view projection matrix, and the corner points of the far plane are determined by finding the intersections of the planes. While rendering, the corner points of the far plane are used to update the vertices and thereby enabling stitching. Beside the corner information, the vertex buffer also consists of homogeneous UV-coordinates.

In Figure 3.11, a camera with the corresponding far plane inside a virtual environment is shown. The far plane of the camera is used to stitch the image onto a cubemap in each frame while running the application to enhance the environment lighting. Inside the background, a partially filled cubemap is shown. The current image stream is stitched into the cubemap by using the far plane of the camera. The FoV of the image stream is included inside the intrinsic camera parameters and is part of the view projection matrix. In the background, the currently stitched information in the cubemap is displayed as the skybox which looks blurry because of the resolution of the cubemap.

Figure 3.11 The image stream (lower right corner) is projected onto the camera's far plane. It is rendered with alpha blending into the already (partially) filled cubemap. Thus, it is possible to fill the cubemap at runtime by combining current and previous results while moving the camera. (This Bedroom 3D model is licensed under CC Attribution-ShareAlike, https://sketchfab.com/models/869e6ec859a84240b9a099ae829f47fa, accessed 25.03.2020)

Curved Plane

A reconstruction using the camera far plane may leaves many empty areas (black parts) inside the cubemap. To deal with this issue, a physical incorrect geometry has also been tested. Hereby, the idea of a curved display was taken into account, whereby the camera is the sweet spot and the image is around the viewer. As a result, using a geometry covering nearly 180-degrees showed to be suitable in some testings where the environment is not too complex.

Similar to the previous approach that used the camera far plane, the curved plane is also defined by homogeneous texture coordinates ranging from $P_0(0, 0)$ to $P_1(1, 1)$ and the current camera image is stitched onto the cubemap directly via these texture coordinates. The curved plane is assumed as an omni directional geometry in the origin of the coordinate system. Accordingly, the geometry is transformed on the basis of the camera parameters. Equation 3.6 illustrates the mathematical background with R as the rotation of the view matrix, and D the distance between the camera position and the coordinate system origin. This transforms the curved plane into the correct position and the current camera image can be combined with the cubemap.

$$PM = R^T * T(0, 0, D) \qquad (3.6)$$

The usage of a curved plane was not sufficient to achieve a good visual reflection. The problem was that the overlapping part was too big in each frame which leads to a blurry result in the combination step. So, the curved plane has been neglected and the camera plane of the previous technique has been used in further research.

Combination
After capturing the image stream, the information needs to be saved in the cubemap. So, the currently existing information in the cubemap needs to be combined with the current frame/image. Therefore, a rendering is needed which is efficient and leads to correct results.

Rendering onto the cubemap, in this approach, is achieved with a single draw call using the geometry shader stage. During the execution of the application, an increasingly enriched cubemap is generated by continuously applying the most recent data of the camera image stream. The sampling of the camera image is determined by the homogeneous texture coordinates of the geometry. A pixel shader combines the camera images after applying a simple alpha blending towards the edges of the camera image The alpha value is linearly interpolated in such a way that the new image information is almost transparent at its borders. This improves the overall result of the stitching between new and previous information, thereby making the reflections more homogeneous. Equation 3.7 shows the calculation of the alpha value for the alpha blending.

$$V_{UV} = -1 + 2 * UV$$
$$R = \sqrt{V_{UV} \cdot V_{UV}} \tag{3.7}$$
$$A = \max(0, \min(1 - R, 1) * B)$$

The current texture coordinate UV is used to calculate the linear interpolation from the center to the border. The longer the camera is not moving and rotating, the more information is saved inside the render target. B is a bias to manipulate the influence of the alpha channel — a higher value means that more information is added, while a smaller value ensures smoother transitions. However, details in the image can be lost with a smaller value. A value of 1.4 was found to be optimal in several test runs.

The lighting in front of the camera is available immediately when starting the application. However, most parts of the cubemap representing the reflections are still empty (i.e. black or predefined) as they have not yet been visible for the camera. In first tests, these areas were filled with information of the precalculated LUT allowing for complete lighting. Some cracks became visible because of the non-realistic approximation using the LUT close to the image border of the stitched information. Unfortunately, the plausibility of the environment illumination suffered severely.

As already mentioned, due to the local behavior of a light probe, the lighting of a cubemap may only be reconstructed for a specific location in space. In this approach, the coordinate origin serves as the starting point for further calculations but any other location may be used instead which has to be taken into account. Ideally, the camera is at the same point as the center of the cubemap that is created in the first frame and should only perform rotations to enable perfect stitching. Usually, the transformation of the camera typically includes a movement and the camera is mostly not in the center of the cubemap which raises a problem when stitching because previous information was created from different viewpoints. Thus, stripes and artifacts are visible in the cubemap, which is particularly noticeable when the camera is moved very quickly. For the evaluation, a perspective transformation of the camera image into the intended area was tested depending on the viewing angle of the cubemap. Therefore, the far plane has to be transformed by a perspective warp and the result stored in the cubemap without alpha blending. The output show large gaps and some cracks in the final result caused by the perspective warp. As a result, the output is disrupted by many artifacts, and hence, it is generally worse than simple stitching with the camera far plane.

The resulting environment map allows a realistic reflection on smooth, mirror-like surfaces as soon as the entire environment has been captured once. Figure 3.12 shows two stitched panorama with many visible areas. On the left side, an alley is recorded and the right side shows an outdoor situation on a sunny day.

The final environment consists of far-field illumination based on the surrounding environment. In both panoramas, it can be observed that the reflection on a mirror-like surface provides even detail information about the environment. The result is a virtual texture of the environment based on the far-field illumination in reality. Stitching can even be used to visualize detailed information from the environment on mirror-like surfaces.

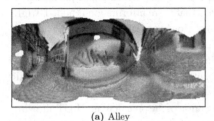
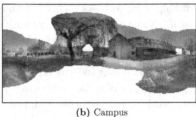

(a) Alley   (b) Campus

Figure 3.12 The environment can be captured by using an image stream in combination with tracking data. (a) shows an alley and (b) an outdoor environment. These are two results of a stitched environment using an image stream in combination with tracking data. The top and bottom part of the projection is essentially white

3.2.4   Estimation with Neural Network

The main problem with the stitching approach using a default camera are missing areas in the panorama data. Areas that were not captured by the camera remain undefined or black in the environment map. As a first assumption, the LUT was used to fill up these gaps, whereby hard edges between the LUT and the stitching became visible.

In the case of creating environment maps, a more sophisticated solution is needed that takes previously captured lighting into account. This approach should take care of the environment and create highly realistic results in realtime. The solution here is to use a neural network with an unsupervised feature learning algorithm driven by context-based pixel prediction [108]. The most related approach by Pathak et al. [89] shows a CNN which was trained to generate unknown content within an arbitrary image region. The authors of this approach stated that the network is even capable to do semantic inpainting. So, this perfectly fits the requirement of the estimation of unidentified areas in the environment lighting.

Architecture: The neural network approach uses a GAN architecture with a generator and discriminator following the suggested implementation by Pathak et al. [89].

The generator downsamples the input data five times while increasing the number of filters at the same time. After downsizing, a 2D convolution with 4000 filters is applied whereby different filter sizes have been tested — a value of 4000 shows to be the most promising regarding the results. Afterwards, the result is upsampled five times until the input size is reached again while decreasing the number of filters back to the three input channels (RGB). While downsampling, a leaky version of a Rectified Linear Unit (ReLU) with an alpha value of 0.2 as activation function is used. In each upsampling layer, the non-leaky version of ReLU with an alpha value of 0.2 has been selected. A graphical visualization of the generator is shown in Figure 3.13.

The result of the generator is used as the input for the discriminator to identify the quality in comparison to the ground truth while the discriminator uses a 2D convolution resulting in a single value that indicates the quality of the panorama. More information is provided in the electronic supplementary material Chapter G with a detailed look into each layer.

Training: The generator is trained by many different equirectangular panoramas with some undefined areas as input. Based on this input data, the generator estimates results with filled areas/patches which will be further processed in two different ways. First, a pixel-wise loss is calculated from the input image and the estimate. In addition, second, the discriminator evaluates to what extent the estimated image

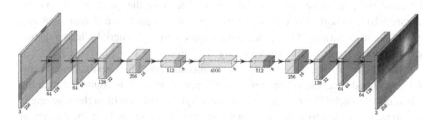

Figure 3.13 The generator downsamples the input, identifies different filters and scales up to the input resolution. In the beginning, an example image from the training data is shown. After processing the data in each layer of the neural network, the final output is shown at the end of the pipe. The output of the generator shows to be sufficient for different environments. Later, the result is used for the input of the discriminator to identify the quality of the output in comparison to the ground truth

corresponds to a real panorama. This results in two loss values, which are now combined to a single one. The combination of the values varies between different approaches, whereas within this thesis the pixel-wise loss has the largest influence. The statement of the final loss value is equivalent to the quality of the estimation from the generator.

About the discriminator: It is trained with generated and real panoramas. Through this training, the neural network can later decide how close the generated data comes to a real or artificial panorama. As soon as the result of the generator is close to real data, the discriminator's loss value will be low.

Training data: The SUN360 panorama database by Xiao et al. [120] with high-resolution panorama images grouped into different places has been used. The database consists of 67569 images which are either outdoor or indoor environment maps. Before using this data to train the network, every panorama is scaled to a resolution of $256 \times 128\,px$. Moreover, a generated mask is applied to create some white areas in the panorama. With the mixed reality application context in mind, the training data should be close to real-world data. For training the neural network, Perlin noise [90] is used to generate masks. The idea is to comply with the behavior of a stitched image as good as possible. In Figure 3.14 the applied masks are shown for six different panoramas.

Pipeline: The general pipeline of the GAN using the panoramas is demonstrated in Figure 3.15. As already mentioned, before training, Perlin noise [90] is added to the original panoramas which are the white masks that have to be filled by the generator. As already mentioned, the final loss is calculated by combining the adversarial loss and the pixel-wise loss — which is used to train the generator. Moreover, Figure 3.16 shows further outputs of the generator regarding different light and environment situations. In the electronic supplementary material Chapter I, two results are selected to show a more enlarged version.

After the environment is estimated, the result can be used for visualization. There-fore, as already mentioned, the result of the neural network is combined with the stitching approach. The missing environment light estimation from the stitching is enhanced by the data from the neural network, or to be more precisely the estimation of the neural network is used as the basis and the stitching result is added with an alpha blending. Thus, the result of the neural network with the stitching can than be used as an environment map and enables reflections in MR applications. The amount of already stitched data is less important but the more the environment is known, the better are the results estimated by the neural network.

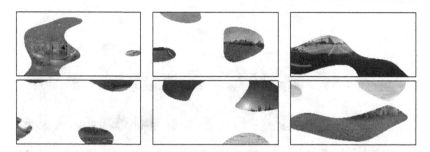

Figure 3.14 These examples show panoramas of the database used as test data. For each panorama, some white masks are added to test the result of the neural network. These white masks are generated by using Perlin noise

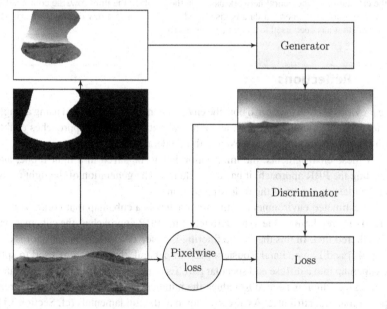

Figure 3.15 The pipeline shows the processing of the data. A panorama with white areas by a Perlin Noise is the input for the generator. The generator estimated an environment based on the input data. Later different loss values are calculated and combined to train the generator

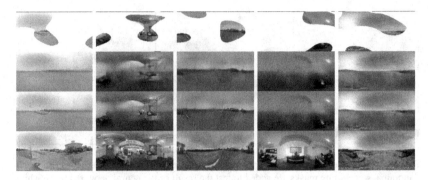

Figure 3.16 In the first row, the panoramas have white areas from Perlin noise. The next row is the estimation of the neural network based on the input. In the third row, the combination of existing data and generated data is visualized — while the last row displays the original panorama that has been used to estimate the loss/error

3.3   Reflections

The previous section explained how the environment can be estimated using a single camera with a stitching approach and a neural network. These approaches enable high-quality environment maps even with fine details inside the reconstruction. To render these environments, the information has to be saved in a light probe, and regarding the PBR approach, it has to be filtered. The generation of the light probe and the filtering is part of the following section.

The estimated environment of the approaches is a cubemap that could be used instantly for rendering. Due to modern real-time PBR approaches, the cubemap has to be filtered first. In this thesis, the filtering is based on the approach by Iorns and Rhee [42] and Lagarde and Rousiers [62]. In general, the filtering is used to split the cubemap into a diffuse and specular part. Each part is precomputed and updated if necessary which is needed to reduce the number of samples regarding different types of material attributes. As already shown in the fundamentals (cf. Section 2.1), a rougher material needs to sample more incident light directions compared to a glossy material.

At first, a low resolution diffuse part for general lighting is generated. Next, a glossy part with individual roughness values for each mip level is calculated. In each mip level, the light information of different material roughness values is predefined and stored. Thereby, a fast calculation of reflection properties can be guaranteed.

The filtering of this approach is based on the work by Lagarde and Rousiers [62] while further information can be found in Karis [52] and Iorns and Rhee [42].

Filtering Glossy: In the real world, many materials have a metallic or glossy surface. The reflections of these materials are based on the material properties — the rougher a material, the blurrier is the reflection. The computation of the incoming and reflected light for each point on the surface is very expensive. Relying on a precomputation might help to decrease computation needed during runtime.

The roughness value is not enough for filtering the lighting because the reflection also depends on the view angle which implies that the cubemap needs to be pre-integrated for glossy reflections using, for example, a microfacet BRDF. As shown by Karis [52] and Lagarde and Rousiers [62] a split-sum for filtering the light probe is used which decompose the BRDF into a DFG and an LD term.

$$
L(v) \approx \underbrace{\frac{1}{N} \sum_{i}^{N} \frac{F(v, h, f_0, f_90)G(l, v, h, \alpha)}{\langle n \cdot v \rangle \langle n \cdot h \rangle}}_{\text{DFG}} \underbrace{\frac{1}{\sum_{i}^{N} \langle n \cdot l \rangle \sum_{i}^{N} L(l) \langle n \cdot l \rangle}}_{\text{LD}} \tag{3.8}
$$

The DFG term can be computed once for every light probe while the LD term needs to be computed for each light probe but the exact derivation is out of the scope of this thesis. To this point, it is enough to emphasize that the DFG term is a 2D function with roughness α and view angle v. So, the DFG term is precomputed once in a 2D LUT with 128×128 pixels and R32G32B32F while starting the application. The pre-computed LUT is shown in the left part (a) of Figure 3.17. A changing view angle is represented in the y-axis while the roughness is inside the x-axis.

The LD term depends on the lighting. So, a glossy texture is filtered every time as soon as the lighting changes (sun movement, texture update, ...). The result can be stored inside a single cubemap using mip levels. Each mip level of the cubemap represents another roughness value. In this thesis, the glossy cubemap is filtered with 32 samples. Depending on the sample size, the final output be calculated faster but with a loss in visual quality. To further enhance the performance, different glossy cubemap resolutions are supported.

Filtering of cubemaps in real-time frame rates is difficult on mobile devices and desktop PCs. Thus, the filtering cannot be carried out each frame or the resolution needs to be reduced. The evaluation shows that a resolution of 256×256 pixel per face (mip level 0) enables smooth and plausible reflections. This is sufficient for modern mobile devices as well as desktop PCs. Figure 3.17 (b) demonstrates the mip levels of the preintegrated glossy cubemap with some visual results in (c).

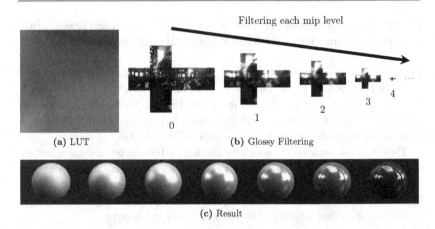

Filtering each mip level

(a) LUT   (b) Glossy Filtering

0   1   2   3   4

(c) Result

Figure 3.17 The glossy cubemap is used for smooth, mirror-like virtual surfaces reflecting the incident light. The size of the cubemap varies depending on the performance and quality. (a) shows the LUT for the computation of the DFG term. (b) shows the importance sampled cubemap with a preintegration of the environment depending on a different roughness value. Part (c) shows seven spheres with different material roughness values. The appropriate mip level of the filtering is used depending on the roughness. (Original cubemap image (b) from http://www.hdrlabs.com/sibl/archive/, accessed 08.04.2020)

Filtering Diffuse: Besides glossy and shiny materials, many different kind of diffuse materials exist in the real world. Therefore, a diffuse filtering needs to be added in order to visualize such materials correctly. To comply with the PBR pipeline, in this thesis, the diffuse Disney BRDF, which depends on the view angle and the roughness of the material [9, 62], is used. Moreover, Filtered Importance Sampling (FIS) by Křivánek and Colbert [58] is used to reduce the number of samples as suggested by Lagarde and Rousiers [62].

This filtering is based on a split-sum importance sampling with 32 samples like the glossy filtering. The generation of the diffuse part can be computed in less than a millisecond even on mobile devises. Hereby the size of the cubemap varies similar to the cubemap for glossy reflections and can be freely adjusted depending on the power of the system. However, a cubemap size of 128×128 pixels per face shows to enable plausible results in AR applications on mobile devices. In contrast to the glossy filtering, only a single calculation is carried out for diffuse filtering, which means that there is no filtering for several mip levels.

The result of the importance sampled cubemap is shown in Figure 3.18 which is related to the same ground-truth cubemap as in the glossy filtering. However, the

Figure 3.18 Applying an importance sampling step a diffuse cubemap can be generated which allows for diffuse lighting of virtual objects in AR

preintegration of the diffuse part can also be done using Spherical Harmonics (SH). More information regarding SH is provided in the electronic supplementary materia Chapter F. In the testings of this thesis, however, importance sampling shows to be sufficient but could be changed in the future by replacing it with SH.

Realization

4

All approaches in Chapter 3 have been explored to enable high-quality visualization in Mixed Reality (MR) applications. Hereby, the visual output as well as the performance for mobile devices and desktop PCs is of particular importance. Therefore, a graphics engine has been implemented using OpenGL 4.5 on desktop PCs and OpenGL ES 3.2 on mobile devices. OpenGL ES is not supported by Apple anymore meaning that the engine supports Windows computers and Android mobile devices. A network-based streaming for remote rendering on Apple devices is included but is out of scope in this thesis.

The main part of this chapter is the realization including the pipeline, techniques, and other technical related issues. Most parts have some pseudocode to emphasize the technical background but also to show data flow and usage. Partly, some more detailed implementations are shown in the electronic supplementary material — especially in Chapter J which also includes source code. The following sections describes the architecture, rendering, light, shadows and the LUT approach, the background estimation with the neural network, and the mixing of the real objects with the virtual scene.

4.1 Architecture

As already mentioned, the engine uses OpenGL with OpenGL ES capabilities in mind. OpenGL ES can be used on mobile devices which is crucial for AR applica-

Electronic supplementary material The online version of this chapter (https://doi.org/10.1007/978-3-658-35192-2_4) contains supplementary material, which is available to authorized users.

T. Schwandt, *High-Quality Illumination of Virtual Objects Based on an Environment Estimation in Mixed Reality Applications*, https://doi.org/10.1007/978-3-658-35192-2_4

tions and for the state-of-the-art approaches. So, this requirement is fundamental to enable high-quality MR on currently available mobile devices.

It is important to note that the architecture of the engine stays the same, regardless of the platform. In general, the engine uses a deferred shading to enable many lights in the scene. Thus, the engine renders every single virtual object into the G-Buffer, which is divided into three RGBA8 buffers holding color, normal, depth, ambient occlusion, reflectance, and metalness information (cf. Section 3.1.2). At first, every visible virtual object inside the frustum of the virtual camera is stored in the G-Buffer during the G-Buffer pass. Estimated real-world surfaces, for example by the SDK, are also added to the G-Buffer. The result of the lighting is stored in a light accumulation buffer (RGBA16F) in the lighting pass which allows HDR. According to the physically-related lighting calculation it can lead to large values stored inside the light accumulation buffer. Therefore, a histogram pass is used to calculate an exposure index which is used to lower the amount of light in the lighting pass. The exposure index of the previous frame is then multiplied with the large lighting values in the current frame. This keeps the float values low (prevent buffer overflow) and offers the possibility of an eye adaption. After this step, a tone mapping transfers the HDR data to LDR in the tone mapping pass. To have a more realistic output, different post-processing effects like SSR, bloom, or anti-aliasing are applied. Some post-processing effects are calculated after the HDR (lighting) pass and some after the LDR pass depending on the technique. Together, all steps represent the basic process of a PBR approach. An overview of the pipeline for rendering on mobile devices and desktop PCs is shown in Figure 4.1.

This overview shows the general structure of the pipeline but the specific sequence of steps within the application is more complex. The specific steps to render virtual objects can be summed up as follows: (1) update light probes, (2) render shadows, (3) collect visible objects and render them into the G-Buffer, (4) calculate the illumination and store it into a light accumulation buffer, (5) render the background/sky/camera image, (6) render transparent objects with light and shadows, (7) apply HDR post-processing effects, (8) compute histogram, (9) apply tone mapping, (10) apply LDR post-processing effects, (11) draw GUI, and (12) finally swap buffer. This can be used for rendering full virtual environments and mixed reality environments with some extra steps. These extra steps are the same as in Figure 4.1: the spatial reconstruction, converting LDR camera image to HDR (inverse tone mapping), and the estimation of environment lighting with creating/updating the light probe.

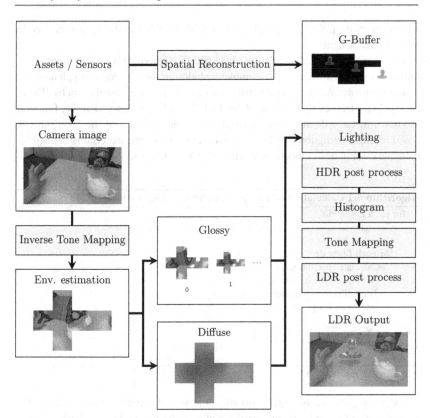

Figure 4.1 This is an overview of the pipeline for HDR AR applications. Sensor data and other assets are used for environment estimation to render highly realistic virtual objects. This pipeline can be used on desktop PC as well as mobile devices

4.2 Physically Based Rendering

Physically Based Rendering (PBR) enables the visualization of a more realistic environment in modern graphics applications. As already pointed out in Chapter 2, the result using physically-based BRDF is very close to those of ray tracing approaches. The basic BRDF of the graphics engine is a combination of Lagarde

and Rousiers [62], Walter et al. [114], and Schlick[104] and the open-source code
of the Unreal Engine[1].

In Algorithm 4.1, the calculation of the BRDF is provided with further information about the used functions and implementation in the electronic supplementary
material Chapter A. The specular part is using a microfacet distribution by Walter
et al. [114], a fresnel algorithm by Schlick [104], and a geometry visibility function
as shown in Lagarde and Rousiers [62]. The approximation of the algorithms is
based on the assumption of physically-based terms like the material is defined by
metalness, roughness, albedo color, and reflectance (as described in Section 3.1.2).

Algorithm 4.1 Calculation of a single pixel for each light with a BRDF

1: **for each** Frame **do**
2:     Get material information from G-Buffer
3:     Get all lights
4:     **for each** Light **do**
5:         Calculate specular term of BRDF
6:         Calculate diffuse term of BRDF
7:         Add both terms together
8:         Add shadowing
9:     **end for**
10:    Set output
11: **end for**

Depending on the material properties, the specular light is influenced by the
metalness term. Like in the real world, non-metallic materials, e.g. plastic, do not
reflect the light manipulated by the material surface color. In contrast, a reflection
on a metallic object is colored by the base color of the surface/material. Therefore,
the algorithm differs between the base color of the material and the specular term
of the material with an orthogonal lighting which can be seen in in Figure 4.2. This
figure shows a glossy plastic (a) and a gold metallic (b) material. It is visible that the
reflection of the environment is manipulated by the metallic specular reflection and,
due to the BRDF, the red color is influencing the reflection. On the left side, the non-
metallic object shows the same reflection highlights but without color changes. The
reflection is still the white material color from the floor that has not been affected.

---

[1] https://github.com/EpicGames/UnrealEngine/, accessed 25.03.2020

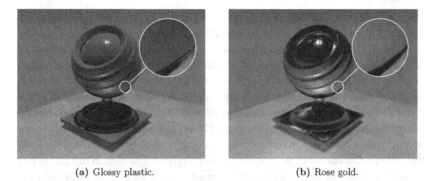

(a) Glossy plastic.   (b) Rose gold.

Figure 4.2 The reflection of the environment is influenced by the color of the metallic material (b). On a non-metallic material (a), the reflection is not influenced

4.3   Light & Shadows

The engine supports different types of light sources including indirect lighting using RSM [16]. In this thesis, a directional/main light and light probes are mainly used while other light sources are used less often.

The main light source in this engine is a directional light with an adjustable direction vector. It is possible to dynamically change the state of the light by changing the direction. In the case of an augmented reality application, this may represent the sunlight in an outdoor environment or the main light source indoors. Hereby, it is possible that the light dynamically responds to changes in the environment. The results in this thesis use ARCore for the main light estimation whereby the light is closer to the real world which leads to more realistic illumination. In addition to the directional light source, point lights or spot lights can be positioned. These are defined by direction, color as well as inner and outer angle and also support shadows. Various types of shadows are supported within the engine, such as hard shadows, soft shadows, and RSM [16] for spot lights. Furthermore, area lights by Heitz et al. [38] are integrated, which are only used for testing purposes without shadow support.

Another important light source are light probes, which in particular have a high influence on the visualization of reflections. The user can set the position of the light probe in the virtual scene, which can be changed at runtime, and the probe collects the ambient lighting. Depending on the desired application, a predefined cubemap (from the file system) can also be used as a light probe or the information from the

environment is determined at runtime (cf. Section 3.2). After the light probe has
captured the information, it can be applied to virtual objects — called IBL. The
position of the light probe and the object is crucial for the calculation because of
the position-dependent reflection. Ideally, the light probe and object is in the same
position to be able to use the information in the light probe directly, although this is
rarely the case. Hence, a correction is applied to solve the parallax correction which
is based on Lagarde [61] (source code to calculate the correction is provided in the
electronic supplementary material Chapter D). In Figure 4.3, the difference between
using parallax correction in comparison to a default calculation is shown. Figure 4.3
(a) shows a non plausible and not physically correlated reflection in the mirror-like
surface. In contrast, the reflection in Figure 4.3 (b) is plausible by applying the
correction.

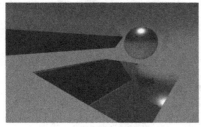 

(a) No parallax correction.   (b) With parallax correction.

Figure 4.3 The parallax correction manipulates the reflecting vector between view and normal which is then be used for texture lookup in the cubemap. On the left side (a) the parallax
correction is turned off and on the right side (b) it is turned on

As already mentioned, reflections can be calculated using light probes in virtual
environments. The same applies to MR applications and the reflection calculations
using the approaches in this thesis. The following sections — as in the previous chapter — calculate an environment map, which is then transferred to a light probe. To
support the visualization of different materials, the light probes are filtered accordingly using different techniques (cf. Section 4.7).

4.4   Lookup Texture

The first environment light estimation approach in this thesis was the reconstruction
of the environment in each frame with the current camera image. In each frame, the

camera image is transformed on a cubemap with a predefined step sequence (cf. Section 3.2.1). The luminance of the environment is stored in the cubemap with an RGB16F format, which can be used for rendering reflections on virtual objects — this is the first approach of this thesis to estimate environment lighting.

The calculation of this estimation is time-consuming if the rendering and filtering have to be done in each frame. Especially, if moving objects are part of the scene, the environment map needs to be refreshed and refiltered every time. To enable dynamic updates of the environment map, a LUT was introduced. Although this does not provide physically correct values, the result is plausible in many scenarios. Especially with complex 3D models in the scene, the representation is often sufficient. In this case, as already mentioned, no inpainting is used and the LUT is calculated once.

The LUT is a cubemap consisting of an RG16F texture (512×512px). Instead of using the image stream of a webcam directly, texture coordinates are used. The resulting texture coordinates for transforming the image stream on the cubemap are stored inside the xy-coordinates of the cubemap, which is then saved as an image file on the file system. In later application cycles, no recalculation is necessary because the image file can be loaded from memory. Only with changes in the values like perspective warp or size of the center part, a recalculation would be necessary. As already mentioned, each pixel of the texture represents a coordinate in the current camera image. At runtime, the texture is stored on the graphics card and a pixel is read depending on the normal of the surface. This pixel corresponds to the incoming light at that position on the surface. In Algorithm 4.2, the texture lookup is shown.

Algorithm 4.2 LUT to calculate related pixel in screen space in every frame

1: Calculate LUT cubemap
2: **for each** Frame **do**
3:    Allocate image stream texture
4:    Fetch texel from LUT cubemap with normal of surface (G-Buffer)
5:    Use texel position to fetch final color from image stream
6:    Set output
7: **end for**

The query is very simple and is only usable for perfect reflective surfaces. For this reason, the LUT and the current camera image are not applied directly to the material. Instead, a light probe is created containing the information of the camera image mapped by the LUT. Likewise, the input is converted from LDR to HDR using inverse tone mapping (cf. electronic supplementary material Chapter C). Afterwards, the light probe is filtered for the diffuse and specular part (cf. Section 4.7).

4.5 Stitching

Reflections with the LUT approach suffer as soon as the reflection is oriented towards the camera/user. In this case, the reflection shows the content visible by the camera instead of the environment that is behind it. To solve this issue, a stitching approach is used to capture the environment while looking around with the camera. In each frame, the image stream of the camera is combined with previous frames.

Based on the current camera image and the camera matrix, the image information is projected onto a cubemap. Technically, a distinction between near and far would be necessary depending on the spatial distance between geometry and camera. However, this distinction is neglected because no depth data are available for identification. Hence, it is assumed that objects are far away from the camera and the results indicates that the visualization is still plausible. Without this distinction, the image information can be interpreted as a global environment map and the information is directly stitched on the cubemap. To further improve stitching, the information is combined using alpha blending which helps to improve the visual quality. Moreover, the rendering of the cubemap is done in a single draw call using a geometry shader allowing the calculation in realtime on desktop as well as on mobile devices using OpenGL ES with geometry shader support (cf. Section 5.3). Algorithm 4.3, describes the basic steps to generate the environment light probe in each frame using the stitching approach.

Algorithm 4.3 Render environment lighting with stitching

1: Extract points   ▷ Far clipping plane extraction
2: Upload points and UV-coordinates to vertex buffer
3: Set cubemap as render target
4: Set camera image as texture
5: **for each** cube face **do**
6:     Update view projection matrix
7:     Render geometry with alpha blending
8: **end for**

Moreover, Algorithm 4.4 shows the fusion of the cubemap and the camera image. With a blending from the camera center to the edges, the cubemap will be enriched further. By that, a smooth blending is possible and the output is more detailed the longer the user does not move the camera. So, blurry results from of a fast-moving camera may be neglected. In the electronic supplementary material Chapter E, a more detailed implementation is shown.

Algorithm 4.4 Alpha blending between a image stream and environment cubemap

---

1: **for each** Frame **do**
2:    Allocate image stream texture
3:    **for each** Side of cubemap **do**
4:        Calculate screen space UV from -1 to 1
5:        Define radius of blending between border and center
6:        Fetch current texel from image stream
7:        Calculate final color based on blending and current frame time
8:        Set output
9:    **end for**
10: **end for**

The stitching approach is the first step before estimating the environment map with the neural network. During running the application, more information is stitched, and by that, the better is the prediction of the neural network.

4.6   Neural Network

Since some image information is missing after stitching, the cubemap is enriched by a neural network. This is done using a Generative Adversarial Network (GAN) which can be used for context-sensitive inpainting. The generator tries to predict a proper environment map while the discriminator judges the result. In combination, the generator learns how to create a more realistic output.

The training of the neural networks depends on the number of batches, number of epochs, and size of the input images. The panorama size of the environment maps is set to $256 \times 128px$ with a RGB8 format. This resolution was chosen because the light probe has a resolution of $128 \times 128px$ and a larger panorama map would not result in a more detailed light probe. A higher resolution for the light probe increases the overall quality but the performance would suffer on mobile devices (cf. Section 5.3).

Training has been done with all 67569 images of the SUN360 panorama database [120]. Further, randomly generated holes — with Perlin noise [90] — are added to the environment maps. The batch size was 16 and the adaptive learning rate optimization algorithm was ADAM with a learning rate of 0.0002. In total, 2000 epochs were scheduled to train the network. The neural network is selected based on the calculated loss value and visual characteristics. With each new lower loss value, the preliminary status of the network was saved together with a selection of results based on the test dataset. The results of the different states of the neural network were then compared and reviewed for image artifacts and plausibility. Algorithm 4.5 shows the process of training the generator and discriminator. Furthermore, the generation of the an output with the generator is shown in Algorithm 4.6 and a more detailed implementation in the electronic supplementary material Chapter E. The communication with the engine is possible by a socket interface that allows the generation as a service like for mobile devices or web applications.

Algorithm 4.5 Training of the neural network

1: Load image dataset
2: Split dataset into train and test data
3: **if** Old model exists **then**
4:     Load previous model
5: **else**
6:     Reset epoch
7: **end if**
8: **for each** Epoch **do**
9:     **for each** Batch in dataset **do**
10:         Add holes to environment map
11:         Convert image to tensor
12:         Generate output with generator
13:         Validate output with discriminator
14:         Calculate adversarial loss and pixelwise loss
15:         Combine losses and optimize generator
16:         Generate real and fake data with discriminator
17:         Calculate adversarial loss based on the real and fake data
18:         Optimize discriminator
19:     **end for**
20: **end for**

Finally, the generated environment map is combined with the currently stitched environment map. This can be done in each frame, depending on the current view of the camera, or the available performance. However, after the environment map has been calculated, it will be stored inside a light probe. As in the other approaches, an efficient filtering of the light probe is necessary.

4.7   Filtering of Light Probes

The information of the environment can be stored inside a light probe to use it for real-time reflection rendering. In this thesis, the information about the environment is stored inside a cubemap — irrespective of which approach is used (LUT, stitching, neural network).

A light probe can be used for diffuse and specular lighting if the cubemap has been filtered accordingly. In this thesis, importance sampling is used for filtering containing all necessary lighting information for diffuse and specular usage. The diffuse information may also be encoded by using SH (cf. electronic supplementary material Chapter G). Depending on the number of SH coefficients, a realistic diffuse lighting can be calculated. Filtering with SH is often used for rough materials only since they have no specular components and a lighting with a diffuse environment map is sufficient. However, as soon as the roughness of the material decreases, a simple diffuse illumination is not sufficient for high-quality reflections. Although SH provides a proper diffuse filtering, the engine in this thesis uses importance sampling for the diffuse term as in Lagarde and Rousiers [62]. The results are sufficient and allow real-time filtering even on mobile devices.

Algorithm 4.6 Estimation of a environment map with the generator

---

1: **for each** Image **do**
2:     Use convolutional 2D layer
3:     Use LeakyReLU activation function
4:     **while** i < 5 **do**
5:         Use convolutional 2D layer
6:         Do batch normalization
7:         Use LeakyReLU activation function
8:     **end while**
9:     Use convolutional 2D layer
10:     **while** i < 6 **do**
11:         Use transpose convolutional 2D layer
12:         Do batch normalization
13:         Use ReLU activation function
14:     **end while**
15:     Use Tanh as activation function
16:     Return result
17: **end for**

The specular part is also filtered by using importance sampling [62]. Here, mip levels of the cubemap are used to precalculate the information for different roughness values of a material. A mip level with a higher resolution is used to fetch samples for smoother materials. Accordingly, a mip level with a lower resolution is used for rougher surfaces. A detailed implementation of the diffuse and specular term is shown in the electronic supplementary material Chapter H.

Filtering of light probes can take some time in the rendering process (cf. Section 5.3) — in particular, the filtering of the specular part is hard to compute in realtime. For this reason, filtering is performed very rarely or precalculated and stored which is more efficient during runtime. However, in a MR environment using the approaches in this thesis, the environment map is continuously changing, and thus it is necessary to carry out the filtering constantly. Therefore, the resolution of the cubemaps in a light probe are additionally reduced depending on the hardware capacity of the output device to ensure real-time capability. A resolution of 128×128 has yielded detailed results on mobile devices without significantly reducing the performance of the application.

4.8   Rendering in Mixed Reality

The combination of the real and virtual world is possible by using differential rendering. The differential rendering allows the representation of shadows, indirect lighting, and other mutual influences between virtual and real-world objects. Conventional differential rendering requires several rendering steps to make this combination possible [17, 65].

In comparison, the approach in this thesis minimizes the number of rendering steps and directly combines the geometry of the real environment with the virtual world. The geometry of the real world is estimated by using the built-in AR framework (in this case ARCore). And in combination with the current image stream, both information (geometry and camera image) becomes part of the G-Buffer (cf. Section 3.1.2). Algorithm 4.7 shows the basic process to store real-world geometry in the G-Buffer.

During the lighting pass, each available geometry and material information is used for further rendering steps including different types of light sources as well as shadows and occlusion. All effects can be achieved with a usual rendering pipeline based on modern graphics engines and applications. If no G-Buffer data is available at a pixel, the lighting is skipped and it is assumed that this is the background information, which is simply the current image stream of the camera in a AR application. A disadvantage of this approach is that the shading of the surfaces results in some visible edges if the material or geometry is not corresponding to the real world. If the virtual geometry does not match the real world, the differences between the

Algorithm 4.7 Transformation of the real world into the G-Buffer

1: **for each** Frame **do**
2:     **for each** Real-world geometry **do**
3:         Upload material properties
4:         Allocate background texture (image stream)
5:         Get UV in screen space
6:         Fetch texel from image stream and use it for albedo
7:         Store material, geometry, and background in G-Buffer
8:     **end for**
9: **end for**

real-world material and the virtual material properties are visible. Although if the virtual geometry fits the real environment, it is not a problem because the material property for the entire surface is changed. Besides, if the geometric approximation is too small, the material properties must be as close as possible to reality. In this case, the calculation of shadows would still be possible without visible edges. However, this is difficult to achieve in complex scenarios.

Accordingly, a technique has been implemented in the engine allowing shadows without using material properties. Therefore, arbitrary surfaces or planar surfaces are also used, but in contrast to the previous technique, the geometry is rendered in the forward rendering pass. By that, shadows are rendered without making edges visible because no material information is needed. Only shadows are rendered and added to the visual output. In Algorithm 4.8, the code for enabling shadows is shown.

Algorithm 4.8 Rendering of shadows in AR using real-world geometry

1: **for each** Frame **do**
2:     **for each** Geometry **do**
3:         Allocate background texture (image stream)
4:         Get UV in screen space
5:         Fetch texel from background with UV
6:         Allocate G-Buffer data
7:         **for each** Light **do**
8:             Get light properties
9:             Calculate attenuation
10:             Accumulate luminance
11:         **end for**
12:     **end for**
13:     Set output
14: **end for**

4.9   Post-Processing

Post-processing effects are widely used. The engine in this thesis provides post-processing effects to allow artists and designer to change and tweak the overall look and feel of the rendering. They change the current image from the viewer's perspective to achieve a specific effect, for example ambient shadowing, depth of field, or bloom effect (HDR blooming effect on bright objects). These methods often work in screen space and use textures from previous stages, such as the G-Buffer.

Inside this thesis, a distinction is made between LDR and HDR effects, which are called at different times in the pipeline. In this section, the implementation of the effects ambient occlusion, screen space reflections, and anti-aliasing will be briefly explained. These three effects have a major effect on the final mixed reality output. All post-processing effects were implemented in the engine with GLSL for OpenGL and OpenGL ES.

4.9.1   Ambient Occlusion

Ambient Occlusion (AO) is a term that represents the amount of exposure of every point in a scene. In other words, how much is a point in space occluded by other objects. The effect is often rendered as part of a post-processing step, which is a common way used in real-time applications allowing a faster approximation of real-world ambient occlusion.

An approximation of the ray tracing approach for rasterization is Screen Space Ambient Occlusion (SSAO) which is a shading method to calculate the environment occlusion in realtime. It computes the shading in the scene depending on the distance between surfaces by using the G-Buffer. The calculation can be done in realtime and can help to avoid computationally intensive global lighting calculations. Screen Space Directional Occlusion (SSDO) is an enhancement of SSAO taking the surface normal direction into account to sample the ambient light and by that, to better approximate global illumination [99]. The idea of screen space ambient occlusion is based on the depth and normal information in the G-Buffer where a hemisphere is spanned on every pixel. Within this hemisphere, random samples are used to check the distance to nearby geometry and to what extent occlusion prevails. The number of samples can vary based on the virtual scene, the artist, and available performance. A code snippet of the graphics engine to calculate ambient occlusion in screen space is shown in the electronic supplementary material Chapter B.

The effect is often carried out after the G-Buffer pass and the result is stored inside it. This helps to calculate shadows during post-processing and avoid unnecessary calculations. The engine in this thesis also stores the ambient occlusion term in the G-Buffer and use it to enable a more realistic output.

4.9.2 Screen Space Reflections

Reflections between virtual objects and the environment are possible by light probes which capture the environment at a certain point. However, if only one light probe is inside the scene, no self-reflections on surfaces are possible. In order to make self-reflections possible, ray tracing can be used which is performed in screen space. The scree-space technique for local reflections is integrated in the graphics engine and is called Screen Space Reflections (SSR) by McGuire and Mara [76].

For each pixel, the material is tested for specular reflection, and if this is the case, a ray is generated. Using the information about scene geometry in the G-Buffer, the ray traverses step by step in screen space and the intersection with the geometry is tested. If an intersection with the geometry exists, the color data at this point is used as the reflection information. A problem with this technique is that it only performs in screen space which implies that areas outside of the current view are not part of the calculation. Algorithm 4.9 shows the basic steps in each frame.

In this thesis, SSR is used for short-range reflections between multiple virtual objects and real-world geometry close to the virtual object. Moreover, reflections of virtual objects in the real environment are possible.

Algorithm 4.9 Render SSR in each frame and build HCB

1: **for each** Frame **do**
2:     Render (virtual/real) geometry into the G-Buffer
3:     Determine SSR surfaces based on roughness
4:     Render reflections on these parts
5:     Accumulate the output on top of the light accumulation buffer
6:     Build the HCB with individual blur stages for the next frame
7: **end for**

4.9.3   Anti-Aliasing

To improve rendering quality, anti-aliasing is added as a post-processing step which minimizes the effect of stairs and flickering due to a low resolution of the final image. In this thesis and the graphics engine, Fast Approximate Anti-Aliasing (FXAA) [71] and (Enhanced) Subpixel Morphological Anti Aliasing (SMAA) citeJimenez2012 are used.

Results

5

The previous chapters outline the approaches, the pipeline, and realization. Based on this, different effects can be achieved like glossy reflections on mirror-like surfaces or the manipulation of real-world geometry.

This chapter presents detailed results and a comparison to baseline techniques which are divided into different scenarios (cf. Section 5.1). Each scenario represents a use case, light type, the environment estimation, and/or the manipulation of the real world. Afterwards, the rendering is highlighted with some information about the platform requirements (cf. Section 5.2). Finally (cf. Section 5.3), some performance measurements for different platforms show the timing of the approaches. Screenshots in this chapter are captured with a desktop PC by using a marker for camera tracking. Other AR results are captured with a mobile device using ARCore for tracking and other findings are intermediate values by the engine.

In addition to the results, a digital appendix is provided with further information (cf. electronic supplementary material Chapter J) which contains additional scenarios, figures, videos, screenshots, source code, executables, and more.

5.1 Scenarios

The engine and the included approaches allow for different output depending on the desired effect which could be the estimation of the real-world main light in the room or an environment light estimation. Some techniques are usable in MR,

Electronic supplementary material The online version of this chapter (https://doi.org/10.1007/978-3-658-35192-2_5) contains supplementary material, which is available to authorized users.

T. Schwandt, *High-Quality Illumination of Virtual Objects Based on an Environment Estimation in Mixed Reality Applications*,
https://doi.org/10.1007/978-3-658-35192-2_5

some in virtual, and some in both environments. Therefore, the different findings and outputs are separated into different scenarios.

Each of the scenario can be combined to produce a more realistic output but, depending on the final application, not all scenarios or effects are needed. Especially the rendering timings need to be considered using multiple effects although many timings will be better in the near future because of better hardware.

5.1.1 Punctual Lights

Point light sources are important for lighting in current graphics applications. This type of light source does not have a physical extend like an area light and it is mostly defined as a 360 degree light source (point light) or a spot light. In the case of a spot light, the light source has a position in space and additionally a direction and an inner and outer angle. Many engines—like the engine in this thesis—subdivide the punctual light source in point and spot light sources for further rendering improvements.

This type of light source can be used in AR as well as in virtual environments. In a virtual environment, the light source can be enhanced by enabling indirect lighting. Inside the engine, RSM by Dachsbacher and Stamminger [16] can be activated for spot light sources. An example of RSM and a spot light is shown in Figure 5.1 with a curtain illuminated by a spot light. Light reflected by the curtain illuminates the other side of the wall.

Figure 5.1 Activating RSM by Dachsbacher and Stamminger [16] allows indirect lighting in a virtual environment. Therefore, a more physical correct GI can be visualized

RSM is turned off in a AR setup because timings have shown that the frame rate drops significantly even on Desktop PCs. To enable GI with indirect lighting, more sophisticated approaches need to be added, which could be LightSkin by Lensing [65] or Delta Voxel Cone Tracing (DVCT) by Franke [24].

Nevertheless, punctual lights can produce realistic effects in AR. In Figure 5.2, a scenario is depicted and shows the effect of a punctual light in mixed reality. In this scenario, the surface of the desk is approximated by a plane provided with material properties corresponding to the real-world material—material properties are, as already stated, adjusted manually by the user. In addition, a tablet computer is placed in the scene with an associated virtual geometry and material information. Now the point light illuminates the virtual and real scene, whereby both worlds are taken into account accordingly by the fusion in the G-Buffer. It is important to mention that the resulting specular reflection is different depending on the material information as shown in Figure 5.2.

5.1.2 Directional Light

Besides punctual lights, directional lights can be used for more complex lighting of the scene. Directional lights simulate the light emitted by a light source infinitely far away from the scene, which is comparable to the sun in the real world. The directional light source is defined by a direction without a specific world-space position. Therefore, the light rays of the source are in parallel and the calculation of the shadow is the same as with the spot light but with a orthographic camera. However, the directional light has a huge influence on the visualization of a virtual

(a) Original.   (b) Point light.

Figure 5.2 On the left side (a) the real scene is shown while the right side (b) shows the virtual light source as a punctual light. The point light source is the only light source in the virtual scene. Different specular reflections are shown based on the material properties in the G-Buffer and the light source. (Original image by Schwandt and Broll [107])

environment. Most engines use a directional light as the main light or sun in the environment whereby the sun direction is used to estimate the skybox of the scene. Thus, a direction closer to the horizon causes a sunset or sundown in the virtual environment.

In Figure 5.3 the influence of a directional light on a fully virtual environment is shown. Without the directional light, the scene does not look plausible (a)—the only lighting is from the environment. With an activated directional light, shadows appear and the scene looks more realistic (b). Depending on the sun's position, orientation, intensity, and color, the environment and shadows are visualized. The attributes can be changed via a script or defined by an artist.

(a) Environment without directional light. (b) Environment with a directional light.

Figure 5.3 On the left side (a), a virtual environment with a deactivated directional light is shown. On the right side (b), the directional light is activated. Shadows become visible and the lighting looks more plausible

The same is valid for a mixed reality setup. Like in the previous scenario, a plane is used to represent the ground with a proper material attached. A directional light is facing the scene and illuminates the virtual objects, which can be defined manually or automatically via a script inside the engine's editor. In Figure 5.4, the lighting is shown inside a MR setup with properly illuminated virtual heads within the scene that cast plausible shadows on the ground. The directional light—or main light— is automatically estimated by using ARCore and the direction and intensity are set to the light source properties. This enables a more realistic impression because orientation and intensity are related to the real world. Moreover, specular reflections are possible enabling realistic shiny materials like metallic surfaces (Figure 5.4 (a)) or smooth plastic (Figure 5.4 (b)).

(a) Golden metallic surface.   (b) Glossy plastic surface.

Figure 5.4 A directional light casts a shadow onto the ground. The direction and position of the directional light is estimated by using ARCore. Thus, depending on the real position of the sun, the position of the shadows of virtual objects also changes

5.1.3   Area Lights

Area lights have a physical extend in comparison to punctual or directional lights. In the real world, any light has a physical extent but in a virtual world, this calculation is more complex which leads to a trade-off between performance and realism. Mostly, an area light emits light inside the scene based on a rectangular plane. This plane is defined by a width and a height which means, that it can represent rectangular areas like monitor screens or televisions. Therefore, an image can also be attached to the light source.

However, area light sources are not as efficient as other light sources wherefore point and directional light sources are used mostly. The calculation of the lighting and shadowing is simpler without a physical extent. In this thesis, area lights are implemented according to Heitz et al. [38] without shadows. Figure 5.5 shows two area lights in two different virtual scenes.

(a) Area light with virtual head.   (b) Rotated area light in complex scene.

Figure 5.5 Here, two different virtual scenes are shown with reflections between objects and an area light source. Glossy reflections are calculated regarding the scene geometry and materials

These area lights can also be used in AR which is visualized in Figure 5.6. The reflection on the surface of the tablet computer is based on the use of different virtual geometry—in this case planes—with different material information. Through a plausible configuration of the geometry and material, realistic reflections on the smooth, non-metallic and reflective materials can be displayed. Corresponding to the point light scenario, the area light also shows different reflection types on the surface. In Figure 5.6 (b), the area light is activated and reflections are shown on the tablet and the virtual sphere.

(a) Scene without area light.   (b) Scene with activated area light.

Figure 5.6 In this scene, the real environment has been stored inside the G-Buffer with a virtual sphere and an area light in the virtual environment. According to the area light, the virtual sphere and the real environment are illuminated and the reflection on the tablet shows different characteristics based on the material properties. (a) shows the scene without area light and (b) with the light source turned on. (Original image by Schwandt and Broll [107])

5.1.4 Environment

In the strict sense, the environment is not a typical light source, but rather consists of multiple light information that together defines the environment. This means that in addition to local light sources, all different light events such as reflections are also included. Basically, the environment light usually contains information about the incident light that is far away from the viewer—whereby indoor scenes are also possible at which geometry is closer to the camera. However, finally, the lighting is used to visualize the surroundings on the one hand but also to allow reflections on objects on the other.

There are various techniques to describe the environment in a virtual environment like the use of textures or—a more dynamic approach—the procedural generation of an atmosphere. Figure 5.7 demonstrates the two types of environment lighting using a procedural and textured environment. Regardless of the type, the information is stored in a light probe, which is then used for Image-Based Lighting (IBL). Basically, the higher and more detailed the environmental information is available, the more detailed the light probe is and the more realistic reflections appear. The same applies to mixed reality environments and the representation of virtual objects inside. The following results of the approaches in this thesis highlight the possibilities to approximate the environment and to which extend a high-quality visualization is possible with a single camera. For this purpose, a textured environment is used which is updated at runtime based on the real environment.

(a) Procedural environment.   (b) Textured environment.

Figure 5.7 Environment lighting is important to visualize realistic virtual environments. (a) shows a procedurally generated environment with an atmosphere and (b) uses a texture to define the environment. In both cases, a light probe is placed inside the sphere

Lookup Texture
The result of the LUT is the same as the result of the single camera image approach without inpainting. Therefore, the results of the approach using a single image with inpainting are not part of the chapter. As already mentioned, the inpainting is insufficient and the performance does not fit the real-time requirement on a mobile device (cf. Section 5.3).

In the following, some results using the LUT are shown. As already stated, the stored homogeneous texture coordinates in the LUT can be used to look up the related pixel in the camera image. Regarding the structure of the environment, the LUT is saved as a cubemap. While generating the environment, this texture can be used in a single draw call together with the image stream. So, the generation is very fast and even possible on mobile devices (cf. Section 5.3).

Figure 5.8 shows two examples using the LUT with an estimated panorama. Reflections on the virtual head in the upper row indicates that the approach is a good first assumption for glossy reflections. The panorama in the bottom row is the estimated environment using the LUT depending on the input stream of the upper row (without virtual object).

(a) Scene 1.   (b) Scene 2.

Figure 5.8 The reflection in the virtual head shows the estimated environments. To estimate the environment, a LUT is used to transform the camera image onto a cubemap. The panoramas show the stored information inside the cubemap

In Figure 5.9, another screenshot using the LUT is shown with a virtual cube on a desk. The ball in the real environment is reflected correctly in the left side of the cube. However, depending on the smoothness of the material and the surface of the object, some artifacts—like hard edges—are visible. So, the front of the cube shows a misleading reflection because of the incorrect environment reconstruction. Inside this reflection, the black object and even the plant from the right side are visible (see magnifier).

The visual quality highly depends on the virtual geometry—with more complex geometry, the reflection looks more plausible. Moreover, rougher materials helps to improve the visual quality in general. In Figure 5.11 (a), three different geometries are shown which confirms this finding.

Stitching
The misleading reflections in the LUT approach become very obvious in the case of smooth materials and planar surfaces. With stitching, a more complex environment can be reconstructed—without the disadvantages of using the LUT. Therefore, frame

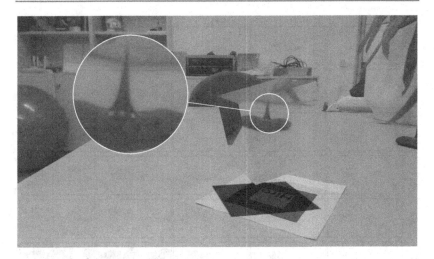

Figure 5.9 The cube inside the scene is illuminated by an environment created with a LUT. At first, the visualization seems to be plausible but a more detailed look reveals some misleading reflections (see magnifier)

by frame, the information of the image stream is stitched together on a cubemap. Depending on the current extrinsic and intrinsic camera parameters, more and more information is stitched onto the cubemap in realtime (cf. Section 5.3).

The stitching procedure can be seen in Figure 5.10. In the beginning, almost no information is available but while using the application more and more information is added to the cubemap/environment. So, after a while, much information about the environment is included in the cubemap and the quality is saturated.

An estimation using the LUT compared to the stitching approach can be seen in Figure 5.11. On the left side (a), the environment is estimated by using a LUT. On the right side (b), the cubemap of the environment is stitched over time. It is clearly visible that the objects in (b) have more plausible reflection information compared to (a). As an example, inside the magnification in the upper row, a telephone from the real world is shown correctly in the stitching technique. In comparison, the reflection in the LUT approach is incorrect. Close range reflections between virtual objects are not visible because the Screen Space Reflections (SSR) effect is not applied.

When enough data has been stitched onto the cubemap, the final result looks plausible and realistic although some information in the environment may still be missing. As a first approach, the missing areas are replaced by using the LUT which leads to some visible errors like cracks and other misleading information. Therefore, a neural network has been used to do a semantic inpainting.

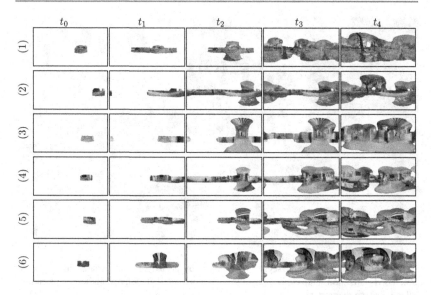

Figure 5.10 These six different environment maps show five states/points in time which were created by the stitching approach. In the beginning, the environment contains only little information. While using the application, the environment is more and more enhanced by using stitching

Estimation with Neural Network

The stitching approach achieves a good visual quality after using the application for a while. However, the technique shows to be insufficient because, usually, not all areas have been captured by the user. Thus some areas are still black if they are not filled by the LUT.

In this case, a neural network can be used for semantic inpainting to fill these areas. Therefore, the network uses 256×128 RGB8 panoramas as input resolution and format with white areas in the panorama which are inpainted later. The estimation with the neural network's generator can be done in realtime (cf. Section 5.3).

In Figure 5.12, a detailed overview of the input and the output data of the neural network is shown. In this figure different scenes are visualized where the upper row shows the current stitching while the bottom row shows the estimation with the neural network. Each column represents a different timestamp while stitching the environment. Figure 5.13 shows the combination of some selected panoramas.

After the semantic estimation of the environment lighting, the results of the neural network are combined with the information from the stitching approach.

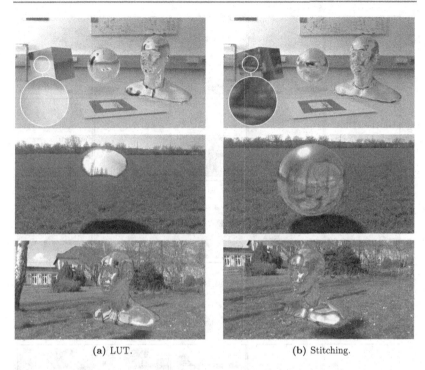

(a) LUT. (b) Stitching.

Figure 5.11 Different scenes with multiple objects are illuminated by an environment light. The left side (a) shows results using the LUT. The right side (b) shows a environment estimated with the stitching approach. In the first row, the environment is prefilled with the LUT. In the second row, the environment is mostly filled by the stitching technique. Empty/black streaks and areas exist due to uncaptured parts. The third row is the stitching approach in combination with a neural network estimation for empty/black areas. SSR is turned off in all cases

A blending is used for the combination, which is based on the alpha value of the stitching. As already mentioned in Section 3.2.3, while stitching, the alpha value is lowered towards the edge of the image information. Thus, a soft edge exists that can be used for the combination allowing smooth transitions between the neural network and stitching results. Figure 5.13 shows the combination with a few selected scenes of Figure 5.12.

On this basis, the lighting is generated according to the current real-world environment. In the final result, there is no visible transition between the stitched image and the generated image due to the blended environment. Figure 5.14 shows screenshots using a light probe of the different scenes from Figure 5.12. These screenshots

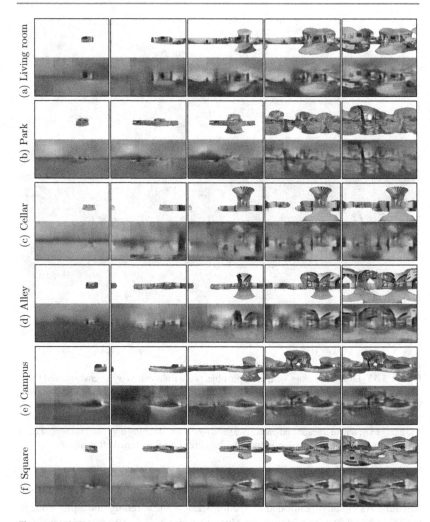

Figure 5.12 Based on the current information, the neural network inpaint white areas which can be seen in the second row. Each scene shows that the more information is available, the better the neural network estimation

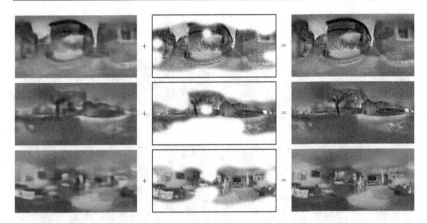

Figure 5.13 The result of the neural network is combined with the currently stitched environment. An alpha blending is used to add the stitching approach to the neural network

visualize a virtual head with a mirror-like material. Some details are clearly visible like the environment behind the camera which has been captured some frames before while moving around with the camera. Other information that has not been stitched so far is estimated by the neural network. So, no hard edges are visible because of the smooth blending between the estimation and the stitched reconstruction.

5.1.5 Manipulation

With the combination of the real and the virtual world into one G-Buffer, a manipulation of the environment may easily be achieved. By changing the approximation with user-defined input, the real world can be manipulated and hereby material and the surface can be changed accordingly. The estimation of the environment can be an approximation or user-defined / non-realistic geometry.

Approximation: Mostly, the virtual scene should be very close to the real environment. If ARCore is available—or any other AR/MR framework that is able to estimate geometry—the detected surfaces (like planes) can be used. In Figure 5.15, an Android mobile device has been used and the detected plane is the approximation of the ground. Hereby, a shadow can be cast on the surface and the scene looks more plausible. Besides, the environment generation using the LUT is enabled.

(a) Living room.   (b) Park.

(c) Cellar.   (d) Alley.

(e) Campus.   (f) Square.

Figure 5.14 These pictures show the result of an environment reconstruction with stitching and neural network. A virtual head is rendered in six different environments. The shadow from the object was created by a directional light which was estimated by ARCore

Non-realistic Geometry: In addition to the technique just mentioned, another possibility is to add virtual objects within the scene that have a different geometry than the real surface. This way, the real world can be manipulated and a variety of effects such as indentations or elevations can be achieved. Figure 5.16 shows the effect of non-realistic geometry with a rock-like object used as real-world approximation. The figure shows how the appearance of the desk changes depending on the surface information. In addition, shadows are correctly represented and follow the physical behavior of the object.

5.2 Rendering

The engine in this thesis supports various types of hardware devices like desktop PC and mobile devices. Therefore, the engine is written in C++ with OpenGL ES 3.2 on mobile devices and OpenGL 4.5 on desktop PCs. It uses PBR to display virtual environments (cf. electronic supplementary material Chapter J) with various post-processing effects which may be applied.

Figure 5.15 Using a plausible approximation of the real environment, visual interactions, like the shadow on the ground, can be rendered

Figure 5.16 By combining the real and virtual world in the G-buffer, different effects can be created. In this figure, among other visual effects, a virtual elevation is added to the desk. For this purpose, only the depth and normal data are manipulated in the G-Buffer. (Original image by Schwandt and Broll [107])

The approaches are included inside the engine except for the neural network. However, this is only for training purposes. Trained networks could be used on mobile devices as well but that needs to be tested in the future. The communication between the neural network and engine is done via a socket connection. So, the neural networks can be used a remote service.

The hardware configuration used for testing was an Android Google Pixel 3 (XL) using ARCore v1.16 for tracking, plane reconstruction, and estimation of the main light. Some other testing was done on a desktop PC with an x64-based Intel Core i7-8700K @ 3.7 GHz, Nvidia GeForce RTX 2080 Ti, and 32 GB DDR4 RAM. To enable AR on desktop PC, the EasyAR framework v2.2.0 has been used with a marker tracking. The neural network is running on the same computer using PyTorch 1.0 for Python 3.7 with CUDA 10.0 for the implementation, training, and testing.

5.3   Performance

Especially in AR scenarios, the performance should be good enough to achieve interactive frame rates. Table 5.1 sums up the timings of the different approaches. The slowest approach is the estimation of the environment using a single camera image while other timings are very fast. All the timings have been measured on the Android mobile device except for the neural network which was tested on the desktop PC. The timings are the mean value over 1000 iterations.

Table 5.1 Performance of the approaches

Approach	Timing (ms)	Timing (FPS)
Single Camera	42.34	24
Lookup Texture	1.63	613
Stitching	1.4	714
Neural network	4.99	200

A draw call of a single image including all rendering steps can also be done in realtime. Filtering the light probe—to enable diffuse and glossy reflections—is the most time-consuming step with 6.02 ms on the mobile device. Other rendering steps are fast and allow for real-time frame rates. To sum up the timings: On the Android mobile device frame rates below 32.25 ms can be provided using the neural network approach with stitching, main light (incl. estimation), filtering, shadows and complex geometry like the head model.

Discussion & Limitations

6

The results shown in the previous chapter highlight the advantages of the approaches for plausible and high-quality reflections in Mixed Reality (MR). All of them can visualize virtual reflections between the real and virtual world in realtime. Even virtual glossy surfaces can be visualized with plausible looking reflections. In addition, a manipulation of the real-world surface is possible by using a novel rendering technique. Results of all approaches indicate that realtime high-quality reflections are feasible on modern mobile devices without using special hardware. Hereby, the physical correctness is less of a problem in comparison to the overall benefit of rendering plausible glossy reflections on virtual objects. The physically-correct rendering is an important step that could be possible with future devices using built-in depth cameras.

In the following, this chapter discusses the results of each approach for the manipulation of the environment and the estimation of the ambient lighting including the single-camera image, LUT, stitching, and neural network estimation. The following parts show the benefits and limitations of each.

Manipulation

The possibilities for rendering high-quality virtual objects in AR depend on the influence of the real environment on the virtual world. However, the virtual world may also influence the real world—like a virtual light source that has different lighting effects based on the real-world surface properties. This is only possible if the real world is represented as realistically as possible in the virtual world. Thus, all shapes, colors, and other properties like material attributes are available, whereby appropriate effects can then be rendered based on these values. There are currently only a few applications that take the influence of the virtual on the real world into account. This thesis shows a possible solution to store the real environment

T. Schwandt, *High-Quality Illumination of Virtual Objects Based on an Environment Estimation in Mixed Reality Applications*,
https://doi.org/10.1007/978-3-658-35192-2_6

in the virtual world in order to use it for lighting but also to manipulate the real environment.

Therefore, data of the real world—together with the virtual world—are stored together in the G-Buffer. A corresponding reconstruction of the real-world geometry and the surfaces is necessary for this. As a first step, 3D models equal to the real surface or detected surfaces by the ARCore SDK are used. However, this may not be sufficient, which is why an improved reconstruction is needed at a later point in time. For now, the current camera image is saved together with geometric data in the G-Buffer. The graphics engine in this thesis uses Physically Based Rendering (PBR) for the visualization of mixed reality worlds. For this reason, material properties are required in addition to the geometry. The shading depends on the material properties (e.g. roughness, metalness) and like the geometry, material properties have to be predefined by the user.

Compared to existing approaches, embedding the real world in the G-Buffer offers far-reaching possibilities without rendering the virtual geometry multiple times. The reconstruction of the environment and the possible adjustment by the user provides the chance to manipulate the environment. Accordingly, different effects can be applied like virtual hills on the real geometry (cf. Section 5.1.5).

Single Image Estimation Approach
Sufficient information about the ambient lighting is necessary to render reflections on mirror-like surfaces. Ideally, the entire real environment is scanned and available as a digital model but this is rarely possible because the digitization of the environment is complex. For example, 3D artists can create a virtual model of the environment which can take several hours or days depending on the complexity of the surrounding. To simplify this process, researchers are looking for solutions based on several cameras in the room, fish-eye lenses, or depth cameras including geometry reconstruction (cf. Section 2.4). In contrast, the focus of this approach and all of the following techniques is on environment light estimation without additional hardware.

The first solution to estimate the environment was to capture the surroundings with the current camera image only (cf. Section 3.2.1). Here, the estimation of the surrounding is updated with each frame and in contrast to previous methods, no additional hardware is required. In each frame, the image taken by the camera is inserted into a cubemap, and at the same time, the estimation of the environment allows moving real-world objects to be taken into account. This means that the user's hand can be seen in the reflection of a virtual object if s/he holds their hand inside the camera view which creates a significant benefit compared to prior approaches. The downside of this approach is that this reflection is only visible if the object (hand) is inside the image of the camera. If the corresponding data is not available, this object is not visible in the reflection. Moreover, a complex computation is necessary for the transformation of the image onto the surrounding cubemap. Thus, the frame rate suffers since the camera image is transformed anew in each frame (42.34 *ms* per frame, cf. Section 5.3). By that, a calculation on mobile devices is not possible using this approach.

In contrast to the current state of research, this approach offers the possibility to display specular reflections in realtime without special requirements like fish-eye lenses [32, 24]. Without the requirement of additional hardware (except a webcam), the technology can be used in existing and upcoming mobile AR applications. Current environment estimations offered by AR frameworks (ARKit, ARCore) also do not require additional hardware but also do not provide detailed reflections. In Figure 6.1, a comparison between ARCore's environment light estimation by LeGendre et al. [64] and the single camera image approach is shown. Side by side, both reflections on the object, which has a smooth surface, are plausible. The ARCore HDR estimation shows a blurry reflection that fits the environment but provides less detail.

(a) LUT.   (b) ARCore.

Figure 6.1 The single image estimation (a) has a much more detailed reflection than the estimation by ARCore [64] (b). Both results show similar colors but (b) is blurrier and darker. As a result, the object does not appear as reflective as it is

Lookup Texture Approach

Based on the previous approach, an extension was introduced in Section 3.2.2. This novel approach provides the same visual output like the single image estimation with some advantages over previous and other approaches.

A cubemap LUT is used for the calculation of the ambient lighting that consists of homogeneous coordinates to allow fast access of a pixel in the image stream. Each pixel is related to a position on the environment (cubemap) and the image stream.

This texture is created once at the beginning of the application's life time or loaded from the file system. As in the previous approach, the result is saved in an environment map and by using this texture, complex calculations of transformations are not necessary at runtime, which leads to a significant improvement in performance. The frame rate is below $2\,ms$ in contrast to $42.34\,ms$ with the single-image-only approach (cf. Section 5.3). However, the approach has some disadvantages like the reflection still consists of the current information inside the camera view only. Previously captured information is not taken into account, which means that reflections sometimes look implausible. In some cases, virtual objects appear more transparent rather than reflective. The results have shown that this is less of a problem with complex objects rather than with simple objects such as spheres or cubes. Figure 6.2 shows a virtual sphere on a sidewalk. The reflection in the sphere is misleading in some cases like the wrong estimation highlighted inside the magnifier. The wheel of the bicycle at the border of the image is transformed into the cubemap so it can be seen twice. Moreover, the wall corner should not be visible because it is behind the sphere.

Figure 6.2 Depending on the surface and the material, the reflections on objects are misleading. They can look transparent like glass like in the magnifier showing wrong reflections

The reconstruction with the LUT is an important step towards mobile environment light estimation. Compared to the state of the art, this approach offers a simple and fast solution for MR applications that provides simple specular reflections (Figure 6.1). In some cases, like in Figure 6.1, the estimation with LUT can be sufficient, for example, when using complex objects, partly glossy surfaces on 3D models, or rougher materials.

Stitching Approach

As already mentioned, an environment can also be recorded by several cameras (cf. Section 2.4.3). If there are enough cameras, the entire environment can be recorded and saved in a cubemap. To avoid using multiple cameras, there is the option of combining the video data of one camera together with the current position and orientation in order to save it in a cubemap—previously and upcoming frames of the image stream are stitched together. This procedure is used in this thesis to enable high-quality reflections for MR applications (cf. Section 3.2.3).

This approach offers the advantage that the environment light estimation contains camera-location dependent data. Thus, it is possible to display objects behind the camera in the reflections of a virtual object, which is also possible with other research approaches but only with a more complex scene setup. Here, the information is stitched together without additional hardware or knowledge about the environment—only the camera image and transformation is used. The image data can be saved in the cubemap in less than $1.4\,ms$ (cf. Section 5.3). Interestingly, while this approach depends on camera movement, this also introduces one limitation: While moving the camera, the offset between two frames produces some artifacts. The movement shifts the viewing angle to the surroundings, which means that previous information may not match the current one although, with the help of a parallax shift, resulting artifacts can be partially removed. In addition, another drawback is that the environment map could be incomplete because it is unlikely that the user will record all areas of the environment with the camera. Correspondingly, black spots arise in the texture as shown in Figure 6.3, which may be filled in with the result from the LUT approach. But using the LUT as the base is not a suitable solution for realistic reflections since there are color differences between the two sources. Then, the boundary at which the images overlap is clearly visible.

Figure 6.3 The stitching approach shows plausible reflections even on simple objects. However, when the camera has not captured some parts of the environment, the reflected area remains black like on the virtual objects in the scene

Besides using a LUT, inpainting can be used to overcome the limitation of missing data. Hereby, the current context has to be taken into account and it should be possible to calculate it quickly.

Estimation with a Neural Network
Nowadays, neural networks are used in a variety of ways like the semantic inpainting of image content. In the case of environment light estimation, this thesis uses a GAN to add missing image data (cf. Section 2.5) to the stitching result.

As mentioned in the previous sections, an image stitching approach often results in areas where data is missing (cf. Section 3.2.4) and an semantic inpainting with a GAN for filling the black areas has been tested. Corresponding results in Section 5.1.4 show that the environment can be plausibly reconstructed using a neural network. The advantage of the neural network in combination with stitching is, that the more information is transferred to the cubemap, the better is the approximation of the approach. Even in the beginning where only a few images have been taken, a plausible reflection can be generated (cf. Section 5.1.4). As long as the user is not moving several meters away from the light probe, the quality of the stitching, in combination with the neural network estimation, is rather good. The reflections on the object's surface are plausible while offering simple rendering. Only the training takes a certain amount of time, but this is not done at application runtime. Image generation took 4.99 ms per frame (cf. Section 5.3), which makes the approach realtime capable even on mobile devices. A drawback of the approach is that the prior training of the neural network makes it impossible to learn further environments during runtime. The network has been trained with a predefined set of training data, which contains both indoor and outdoor scenes. The panoramas in the data set are very versatile, which means that the network creates a good but vague approximation.

(a) ARCore.   (b) Stitching and neural network.

(c) Stitched Environment.   (d) Estimated Environment.

Figure 6.4 The ARCore estimation by LeGendre et al. [64] in (a) looks plausible but the model tends to be rougher because of the blurry ARCore environment light estimation. (b) shows the estimation using the neural network in this thesis in combination with the stitching. (c) shows the stitched environment combined with the neural network estimation in (d)

In Figure 6.4, a comparison between the neural network (with stitching) and the environment estimation by LeGendre et al. [64] is shown. Both applications have seen the same parts of the environment and use the same data to estimate the global light probe. In comparison to the ARCore environment estimation by LeGendre et al. [64], the stitching in combination with the neural network shows to be more promising. Details can be captured while the rest of the environment is roughly estimated by the neural network. Finally, the stitching approach in combination with the neural network estimation is a good approximation offering high-quality reflections on mirror-like virtual objects. In comparison to the AR framework, the approach offers more detailed reflections for MR applications—the estimation with ARCore is blurrier with fewer details of the surrounding. Figure 6.4 (d) shows the estimated environment with the neural network. In some cases, the estimation with the neural network is not as expected like the black streak on the ground in Figure 6.4 (d), which can be due to various reasons, such as the already mentioned training data. Depending on the object and the scene, these errors in the estimation are more or less noticeable.

The four approaches to estimate the environment light are compared in Table 6.1. This overview shows the approaches and compares them in terms of performance, reconstruction time, flexibility, and the use of two different object types for visualization. Herby, simple objects are spheres and cubes and complex objects are, for example, the head that has been shown several times in this thesis. The symbols mean: + condition fulfilled, / sufficiently fulfilled and − with exceptions fulfilled.

Table 6.1 Comparison of environment light estimation approaches in this thesis. (T1 = Performance; T2 = Reconstruction; T3 = Flexibility; T4 = Simple object; T5 = Complex objects)

Approach	T1	T2	T3	T4	T5
Single camera	/	+	+	−	+
Lookup Texture	+	+	+	−	+
Stitching	+	−	+	/	/
Neural network	+	/	/	+	+

All approaches can be used in mixed reality applications. Only the single-camera approach does not meet a sufficient frame rate to be used in realtime. Reconstruction is possible with the single camera and LUT approach from the first frame. The stitching approach needs some time since the surroundings first have to be recorded. An inpainting with a neural network makes an estimation possible from the first frame, but with restrictions in the level of detail. The first three techniques can be used regardless of the environment which implies that they are flexibly usable. The neural network is limited at this point since the quality of the network depends on the training data. Depending on the type of virtual objects, the approaches show their advantages and disadvantages. Using simple objects, problems with reflections can be noticed quickly except the stitching (if sufficiently filled) and the neural network approach. Complex objects are generally less of a problem for all approaches.

Compared to other existing approaches, all four variants offer the advantage of not requiring any additional hardware. At the same time, reflective information of the environment can be rendered on different materials and geometries in mixed reality. Thus, the approaches in the thesis solve issues of previous state of the art like Debevec [17] since no special objects have to be placed in the scene. Furthermore, there is no need for a depth camera or special lenses to capture the lighting as in Grosch, Eble, and Mueller [32], Franke [24], Gruber, Ventura, and Schmalstieg [34], and Richter-Trummer et al. [97]. Besides, some research [34, 97] focus on the reconstruction of diffuse lighting only. Approaches such as those by Karsch et al. [53] enable detailed glossy reflections, but no dynamic environments can be provided, especially if they are too complex and largely different from the environment maps in the digital library. Related approaches like Ropinski, Wachenfeld, and Hinrichs [101] and Chew and Lian [10] do, in contrast to the approaches in this thesis, either not allow sufficient performance or are not suitable for unrestricted camera movement in mixed reality. Moreover, the main issue with stitching [10] are holes in the reconstruction, which is addressed by using a semantic inpainting in this thesis.

Conclusion & Outlook

7

This thesis introduced various approaches to estimate the environment, manipulate the spatial behavior, and create different lighting effects between the real and virtual world. The main contributions of this thesis are (1) a real-time rendering for MR applications combining real-world and virtual content in the G-Buffer, (2) a manipulation of the real world by adjusting material and geometry properties, and (3) an environment reconstruction with different methods like a context-sensitive inpainting on a partly captured lighting.

Rendering

Each rendering method can be calculated in realtime on a common desktop PC as well as on mobile devices. Thus, the approaches can be used in various application domains. However, filtering of the environment cubemap is still a problem in case of real-time requirements. Filtering one texture is only possible with modern devices but performance decreases as soon as multiple light probes are inside the scene. In the case of a far-field illumination, only one environment cubemap is necessary, although by adding virtual objects inside the scene, multiple light probes are needed for local reflections. Thus, multiple cubemaps need to be filtered, which can be compensated by splitting the cubemap into local and global light probes. In a mixed reality setup, the global light probe is updated for every frame and filtered afterward. Any local light probe is marked as static and has to be updated only as long as an object is moving. After that, the light probes are blended and combined to calculate the reflection.

Future Work: By supporting further light probes, interesting new research questions could arise in the future. It would be possible, for example, to support local reflections without using SSR. Accordingly, new strategies for filtering are necessary that ensure real-time capability. Besides, the implementation of additional

T. Schwandt, *High-Quality Illumination of Virtual Objects Based on an Environment Estimation in Mixed Reality Applications*,
https://doi.org/10.1007/978-3-658-35192-2_7

post-processing effects would further increase the overall quality by supporting, for example, depth of field for mixed reality. Another very interesting step would be the implementation of ray tracing to enable lighting effects such as indirect light or caustics. In general, ray tracing could provide higher quality and physically correct output in MR. Current applications requiring high-quality lighting can already benefit from the rendering in this work.

Manipulation
This thesis shows an approach to manipulate the real environment by transferring the real into the virtual world. Therefore, the real and virtual environment are combined into a G-Buffer, which can be freely manipulated to render different effects that consider shading, lighting, reflections, and physical behavior. Light sources can be rendered without using extra draw calls as common differential rendering approaches do. Moreover, different light sources can easily be integrated to enhance the visual quality of the application. Besides, by defining the material of a real-world surface, the effect of the lighting is different: so, the specular reflection looks different on smooth surfaces in comparison to rougher surfaces. In addition, the adjustment by the user offers the possibility to have a real-time manipulation of the environment for the virtual as well as for the real world.

Future Work: In the future, more sensors of a mobile phone could be used (e.g. LIDAR sensors, or built-in depth sensors). By using additional sensors, it would be possible to record complex real-world geometries and at the same time, the sensors could also be used to detect materials. Thus, it would enable an improved visualization and further manipulation possibilities. In general, a more advanced capture of the real world even offers the possibility to remove objects—a 3D diminished reality approach. However, a different data structure would be necessary for this, for example, a G-Buffer with multiple layers or a voxel structure.

Environment Light Estimation
The first approach in this thesis is the estimation of the environment by using just a single camera image. In each frame, the image stream is mapped onto a cubemap which can be used for rendering virtual reflections later. Using the single camera image of a common input device—like a webcam or a mobile phone—is appropriate as a first estimation. Reflections on virtual objects inside the scene are plausible by using the input stream for foreground and background illumination. Compared to other approaches, this offers the advantage that no additional hardware is required and even moving objects are visible by using the single camera image.

However, the performance of this approach is a major drawback. Thus, the basic steps to transform the image onto a cubemap have been stored inside a lookup texture. Inpainting is neglected and heavy calculations are precomputed by using a cubemap LUT which allows much faster rendering while the output is similar. Reflections are still plausible and moving objects are detected immediately even on mobile devices with high frame rates. It is important to note that this technique can be used widely for various MR applications as it does not require special hardware.

The LUT approach still has the disadvantage that reflections can look implausible especially with flat mirror-like surfaces directed towards the camera. By using a stitching approach the information of the environment is captured using the camera image in combination with the tracked position and orientation which enhances the plausibility of the reflections. In every frame, the information is stitched onto a cubemap and can be rendered within a single draw call. As soon as the environment has been captured, a plausible and realistic environment map is generated. Thus, reflections on simple and complex virtual objects look more plausible in contrast to the LUT approach. In the future, this approach needs to be improved to handle the case of a fast-moving camera producing blurry results which could be overcome by considering the movement speed of the camera. Moreover, the projection of the camera can produce false results as soon as the position of the camera has a longer distance between the position of the light probe and the current position. The results are hard edges, smearing and other discrepancies which can be overcome by either using an advanced parallax correction or multiple light probes.

A drawback of stitching is that the user will usually not record the entire environment to use the AR application, which means that parts of the environment are not stored in the cubemap. To fill these empty parts, a neural network is used in the fourth approach which estimate a context-sensitive environment. The combination of the stitching approach and the estimation by the neural network allows the generation of a sufficient environment map which can be used for ambient lighting. A complete environment is estimated without hard edges and even background reflections are possible. However, to visualize the reflection of the background, the information has to be seen at least once by the camera. Also, the estimation by the neural network is only as good as the data of the stitching. This implies that the approach is insufficient at the beginning but improves as soon as more data is available.

Future Work: A possible future work would be the issue of the local correspondence between the light probe and the camera position. Usually, the user is moving around while using a MR application but in this case, the stitching breaks as soon as the user is moving too far from the origin of the light probe. A solution would be multiple light probes embedded inside the scene with the correct stitching information based on the camera position. The estimation could be done for each light probe in the scene and these could be blended by considering the distance to the object and the camera. Moreover, each light probe might be intelligently positioned by using artificial intelligence analyzing the environment. Thus, even more complex lighting setups are possible.

Another potential future work would be the use of additional sensors such as the front camera in a smartphone, which would accelerate the performance when determining the environment lighting. However, it should be noticed that the front camera usually captures the user's face which must not be taken into account while stitching. Furthermore, the use of two cameras in the same smartphone is currently not supported with the SDK but has been announced for future versions.

Concerning the neural network, another improvement would be the use of HDR which may be beneficial for the PBR pipeline. Instead of generating HDR environments directly, the LDR could be converted to HDR by using another neural network. Initial tests showed that this method, in contrast to the current inverse tone mapping, produces promising results which allow for a fast environment light estimation within the first frames of the application.

A further improvement of the estimation quality would be to train the neural network beyond the training phase. Thus, the network could be trained with every intermediate stitching result until the complete environment map is known and the network can continue to learn even more environments. Besides, the neural network could be improved by supporting image-to-image translation to allow for more detailed reflections. Therefore a digital library could be used to search for a suitable environment map, which could then be used by a neural network for the translation from the coarse to a more detailed environment map.

The approaches in this thesis enable the visualization of high-quality reflections on virtual objects depending on the real environment. Each approach could improve existing applications and therefore expand more than just the scientific contribution. Thus, a user study would be necessary to examine the integration of the approaches in various areas of application.

Conclusion

The research question at the beginning of this thesis was: *To which extent may a seamless integration of visual content into the real environment be achieved for AR?* Four different approaches were presented in the thesis to enable high-quality visualization of reflective surfaces—single image estimation, LUT, stitching, and the estimation with a neural network. The results of each approach indicates that the answer depends on the application. A proper environment estimation is a trade-off between performance, the possibility of immediate usage, and visual quality:

smoother surfaces require a more detailed environment estimation because reflections are potentially more visible, while rougher objects benefit from diffuse lighting reconstruction. In addition to that, the geometry of the model is highly important—more complex objects are less prone to implausible reflections rather than simple geometries. To sum up, a combination makes sense when comparing all approaches. At the beginning of the application, the environment could be estimated by a neural network, and later it is expanded by the camera image information to provide more details.

All approaches in this thesis offer great potential for future work and further research in the research area. The simplicity of implementation and the versatile usability allow interesting new research questions to be opened and to be continued in the future.

Glossary

Ambient Occlusion (AO) is a shading method used in 3D computer graphic applications to calculate the amount of exposure at each point in a scene for ambient lighting.

Android is a SDK and an operating system for mobile devices like mobile phones, TVs, or tablet computers. It has been invented by Google and especially the operating system is installed on many devices nowadays.

ARCloud is a synonym for data exchange between different AR applications. The information in the cloud can be used for communication, orientation, and tracking. Cloud anchors exists while running the application or may be saved persistently in a global cloud for further usage.

ARCore is an AR SDK mainly used on Android devices. The framework includes different algorithms to use the camera image, track targets, and estimate lighting for mobile AR experiences.

ARKit is a AR SDK for Apple devices. It offers almost the same functionality as ARCore to enable AR on Apple's mobile devices.

Asset Assets are textures, shaders, scripts, sound files and everything else that can be used by a engine.

Cubemap is a special graphic texture representing a cube with six faces. Each face is directed towards a cardinal direction. It can be used for environment lighting, reflections, and general data storage.

Deferred Rendering For more information see: Deferred Shading.

Deferred Shading is an approach storing photometric and geometric properties into multiple buffer. This collection of buffers—or textures—represents the information of the environment. For more information see G-Buffer. Based on this G-Buffer, the lighting is computed efficiently allowing multiple lights.

T. Schwandt, *High-Quality Illumination of Virtual Objects Based on an Environment Estimation in Mixed Reality Applications*,
https://doi.org/10.1007/978-3-658-35192-2

Differential Rendering is an approach for the seamless integration of virtual global illumination effects in the real environment. The effect can be achieved by combining both worlds and rendering the virtual environment multiple times.

G-Buffer is a collection of multiple 2D textures which are used for Deferred Rendering. The textures store values like the geometry and the material of the scene based on the current view of the camera.

Global Illumination is the simulation of light behavior between different objects. It contains visual effects like shadowing, (multiple) indirect lighting, caustics and sub-surface scattering. These effects can be computed in real-time or non-real-time applications.

Head Mounted Display (HMD) is a hardware device worn on the head of a user for visualization and tracking. HMDs can be used for AR and VR applications with a display in front of both eyes. Nowadays HMDs are used in different applications like games, sports, medicine, and research.

Inpainting is an image processing approach that can fill missing information. Depending on the neighbor information in the image the approach tries to reconstruct missing areas.

Light Probe provide a way to store incoming light at a certain position in the scene. The light is stored and can be reused for different effects like diffuse or specular lighting.

Lookup texture (LUT) is a texture with information for further processing. In general, lookup textures are precomputed to store preliminary data of complex calculations.

Machine Learning is a collection of functions enabling artificial intelligence. Nowadays, machine learning is used for different kinds of applications like computer vision.

Mipmap is an anti aliasing technique. The resolution is reduced for a texture until the resolution is 1×1 pixel. Each level is a lower resolution of the previous one divided by two.

Neural Network is a machine learning approach for self-learning algorithms. It is based on multiple neurons connected in different ways while each connection has a weight to pass data throw the network. By the end, a complex structure is capable to store many information and process data.

Normal is a vector perpendicular to a surface. With a normal vector, rendering and lighting can be calculated.

OpenGL is a specification of a platform-independent programming interface to communicate with graphics cards. It is used for the development of 2D and 3D applications. Different devices support OpenGL and the embedded system version OpenGL ES.

Physically Based Rendering (PBR) is a special real-time rendering technique emulating the behavior of light. This emulation is based on physically-related formulas to estimate the behavior of light as close as possible to nature. PBR is used in various real-time applications by using different approximations and rendering strategies.

Python is an universal programming language designed for rapid prototyping. Nowadays the programming language is one of the most famous ones. The language has many different packages offering a lot of functionality like machine learning.

PyTorch is an open-source library for Python allowing the development of machine learning approaches.

Render target is a texture—or frame buffer object—used by the graphics card to store the output of a shader. Depending on the graphics framework, this texture can be used for different purposes.

Shader A shader is a small program unit used to manipulate data on the graphics card which can be defined in different stages for data processing like vertex or pixel. Different kind of shader languages exists depending on the graphics framework.

Software Development Kit (SDK) is a collection of program code to support developer. A developer can write code using different SDKs without writing the same code multiple times. Moreover, some hardware requires the use of a SDK to communicate with sensors or internal data.

Spherical Harmonic (SH) SHs are a mathematical model (see Chapter F).

Tone Mapping is the conversion from High Dynamic Range Image (HDRI) to Low Dynamic Range Image (LDRI). Depending on the tone mapping the final output can look different. If the application use HDR, tone mapping is needed to display the final visualization on common output devices. Nowadays most high-quality rendering pipelines use HDR.

Voxel A voxel is a 3D grid point in a 3D structure and is comparable to a pixel in a texture (2D grid). Voxels commonly store spatial structure with position and color information.

Bibliography

1. Michael Adam et al. "Real-time stereo-image stitching using GPU-based belief propagation". In: *Proceedings of the Vision, Modeling, and Visualization Workshop*. Ed. by Marcus A. Magnor, Bodo Rosenhahn, and Holger Theisel. Nov. 2009, pp. 215–224.
2. Charu C. Aggarwal. *Neural Networks and Deep Learning*. Cham: Springer, 2018, p. 497. ISBN: 978-3-319-94462-3. DOI: https://doi.org/10.1007/978-3-319-94463-0.
3. Tomas Akenine-Möller, Eric Haines, and Naty Hoffman. *Real-Time Rendering, Fourth Edition*. 4th. Natick, MA, USA: A. K. Peters, Ltd., 2018. ISBN: 9781138627000.
4. A'aeshah Alhakamy and Mihran Tuceryan. "An Empirical Evaluation of the Performance of Real-Time Illumination Approaches: Realistic Scenes in Augmented Reality". In: *Augmented Reality, Virtual Reality, and Computer Graphics*. Ed. by Lucio Tommaso De Paolis and Patrick Bourdot. Cham: Springer International Publishing, 2019, pp. 179–195. ISBN: 978-3-030-25999-0.
5. Ronald T. Azuma. "A Survey of Augmented Reality". In: *Presence: Teleoper. Virtual Environ.* 6.4 (Aug. 1997), pp. 355–385. ISSN: 1054-7460. DOI: https://doi.org/10.1162/pres.1997.6.4.355.
6. F. Badra, A. Qumsieh, and G. Dudek. "Rotation and zooming in image mosaicing". In: *Proceedings Fourth IEEE Workshop on Applications of Computer Vision. WACV'98*. IEEE, 1998. DOI: https://doi.org/10.1109/ACV.1998.732857.
7. James F. Blinn. "Models of Light Reflection for Computer Synthesized Pictures". In: *Proceedings of the 4th Annual Conference on Computer Graphics and Interactive Techniques*. SIGGRAPH '77. San Jose, California: ACM, 1977, pp. 192–198. DOI: https://doi.org/10.1145/563858.563893.
8. Wolfgang Broll et al. "Authoring von VR/AR-Anwendungen". In: *Virtual und Augmented Reality (VR/AR): Grundlagen und Methoden der Virtuellen und Augmentierten Realität*. Ed. by Ralf Dörner et al. Berlin, Heidelberg: Springer Berlin Heidelberg, 2019, pp. 393–423. ISBN: 978-3-662-58861-1. DOI: https://doi.org/10.1007/978-3-662-58861-1_10.
9. Brent Burley. "Physically-Based Shading at Disney". In: *ACM SIGGRAPH 2012 Course: Practical Physically Based Shading in Film and Game Production* (2012). Ed. by Stephen McAuley et al.

T. Schwandt, *High-Quality Illumination of Virtual Objects Based on an Environment Estimation in Mixed Reality Applications*,
https://doi.org/10.1007/978-3-658-35192-2

10. Victor C. S. Chew and Feng-Li Lian. "Panorama stitching using overlap area weighted image plane projection and dynamic programming for visual localization". In: *2012 IEEE/ASME International Conference on Advanced Intelligent Mechatronics (AIM)*. IEEE, July 2012, pp. 250–255. DOI: https://doi.org/10.1109/AIM.2012.6265995.

11. R. L. Cook and K. E. Torrance. "A Reflectance Model for Computer Graphics". In: *ACM Transactions Graph.* 1.1 (Jan. 1982), pp. 7–24. ISSN: 0730-0301. DOI: https://doi.org/10.1145/357290.357293.

12. Cyril Crassin and Simon Green. In: *OpenGL Insights*. CRC Press, Patrick Cozzi and Christophe Riccio, July 1, 2012.

13. Cyril Crassin et al. "Interactive Indirect Illumination Using Voxel Cone Tracing". In: *Computer Graphics Forum* 30.7 (Sept. 2011), pp. 1921–1930. DOI: https://doi.org/10.1111/j.1467-8659.2011.02063.x.

14. A. Creswell et al. "Generative Adversarial Networks: An Overview". In: *IEEE Signal Processing Magazine* 35.1 (Jan. 2018), pp. 53–65. DOI: https://doi.org/10.1109/MSP.2017.2765202.

15. O.G. Cula and K.J. Dana. "Compact representation of bidirectional texture functions". In: *Proceedings of the 2001 IEEE Computer Society Conference on Computer Vision and Pattern Recognition. CVPR 2001* 1 (2001), pp. 1041–1047. ISSN: 1063-6919. DOI: https://doi.org/10.1109/CVPR.2001.990645.

16. Carsten Dachsbacher and Marc Stamminger. "Reflective Shadow Maps". In: *Proceedings of the 2005 symposium on Interactive 3D graphics and games – SI3D '05*. Association for Computing Machinery (ACM), 2005, pp. 203–231. DOI: https://doi.org/10.1145/1053427.1053460.

17. Paul Debevec. "Rendering Synthetic Objects into Real Scenes: Bridging Traditional and Image-Based Graphics with Global Illumination and High Dynamic Range Photography". In: *Proceedings of the 25th Annual Conference on Computer Graphics and Interactive Techniques*. SIGGRAPH '98. New York, NY, USA: Association for Computing Machinery, 1998, pp. 189–198. ISBN: 0897919998. DOI: https://doi.org/10.1145/280814.280864.

18. Zhao Dong et al. "Predicting Appearance from Measured Microgeometry of Metal Surfaces". In: *ACM Transactions Graph.* 35.1 (2015), 9:1–9:13. ISSN: 07300301. DOI: https://doi.org/10.1145/2815618.

19. Ralf Dörner et al., eds. *Virtual und Augmented Reality (VR/AR)*. Springer Berlin Heidelberg, 2019. ISBN: 978-3-662-58861-1. DOI: https://doi.org/10.1007/978-3-662-58861-1.

20. Ron O. Dror, Edward H. Adelson, and As Willsky. "Recognition of surface reflectance properties from a single image under unknown real-world illumination". In: *IEEE Computer Vision and Pattern Recognition Computer Vision and Pattern Recognition (CVPR)*. 2001.

21. Jakob Engel, Thomas Schöps, and Daniel Cremers. "LSD-SLAM: Large-Scale Direct Monocular SLAM". In: *Computer Vision – ECCV 2014*. Springer International Publishing, 2014, pp. 834–849. DOI: https://doi.org/10.1007/978-3-319-10605-2_54.

22. L. Fei-Fei and P. Perona. "A Bayesian hierarchical model for learning natural scene categories". In: *2005 IEEE Computer Society Conference on Computer Vision and Pattern Recognition (CVPR'05)*. Vol. 2. June 2005, 524–531 vol. 2. DOI: https://doi.org/10.1109/CVPR.2005.16.

23. Nicola Fioraio et al. "Large-scale and drift-free surface reconstruction using online sub-volume registration". In: *2015 IEEE Conference on Computer Vision and Pattern Recognition (CVPR)*. IEEE, June 2015. DOI: https://doi.org/10.1109/CVPR.2015.7299077.

24. Tobias Alexander Franke. "Delta Voxel Cone Tracing". In: *2014 IEEE International Symposium on Mixed and Augmented Reality (ISMAR)*. IEEE, Sept. 2014, pp. 39–44. DOI: https://doi.org/10.1109/ISMAR.2014.6948407.

25. Marc-Andre Gardner et al. "Deep Parametric Indoor Lighting Estimation". In: *2019 IEEE/CVF International Conference on Computer Vision (ICCV)*. IEEE, Oct. 2019. DOI: https://doi.org/10.1109/ICCV.2019.00727.

26. Marc-André Gardner et al. "Learning to Predict Indoor Illumination from a Single Image". In: *ACM Transactions Graph.* 36.6 (Nov. 2017). ISSN: 0730-0301. DOI: https://doi.org/10.1145/3130800.3130891.

27. Stamatios Georgoulis et al. "Reflectance and Natural Illumination from Single-Material Specular Objects Using Deep Learning". In: *IEEE Transactions on Pattern Analysis and Machine Intelligence* 40.8 (Aug. 2018), pp. 1932–1947. DOI: https://doi.org/10.1109/TPAMI.2017.2742999.

28. Stamatios Georgoulis et al. "What is Around the Camera?" In: *Proceedings of the IEEE International Conference on Computer Vision*. IEEE, Oct. 2017, pp. 5170–5178. DOI: https://doi.org/10.1109/ICCV.2017.553.

29. Dan B. Goldman et al. "Shape and spatially-varying BRDFs from photometric stereo". In: *IEEE Transactions on Pattern Analysis and Machine Intelligence* 32.6 (2010), pp. 1060–1071. ISSN: 01628828.

30. Ian Goodfellow, Yoshua Bengio, and Aaron Courville. *Deep Learning*. http://www.deeplearningbook.org. MIT Press, 2016.

31. Ian Goodfellow et al. "Generative Adversarial Nets". In: *Advances in Neural Information Processing Systems 27*. Ed. by Z. Ghahramani et al. Curran Associates, Inc., 2014, pp. 2672–2680.

32. Thorsten Grosch, Tobias Eble, and Stefan Mueller. "Consistent interactive augmentation of live camera images with correct near-field illumination". In: *Proceedings of the 2007 ACM symposium on Virtual reality software and technology – VRST '07*. Vol. 1. 212. New York, New York, USA: ACM Press, 2007, p. 125. ISBN: 9781595938633. DOI: https://doi.org/10.1145/1315184.1315207.

33. Lukas Gruber, Thomas Richter-Trummer, and Dieter Schmalstieg. "Realtime photometric registration from arbitrary geometry". In: *2012 IEEE International Symposium on Mixed and Augmented Reality (ISMAR)*. IEEE, Nov. 2012, pp. 119–128. ISBN: 978-1-4673-4662-7. DOI: https://doi.org/10.1109/ISMAR.2012.6402548.

34. Lukas Gruber, Jonathan Ventura, and Dieter Schmalstieg. "Image-space illumination for augmented reality in dynamic environments". In: *2015 IEEE Virtual Reality (VR)*. IEEE, Mar. 2015, pp. 127–134. ISBN: 978-1-4799-1727-3. DOI: https://doi.org/10.1109/VR.2015.7223334.

35. K. Hara, K. Nishino, and K. Ikeuchi. "Determining reflectance and light position from a single image without distant illumination assumption". In: *Proceedings Ninth IEEE International Conference on Computer Vision* 27.4 (2003), pp. 493–505. ISSN: 0162-8828. DOI: https://doi.org/10.1109/ICCV.2003.1238397.

36. Takahiro Harada, Jay McKee, and Jason C. Yang. "Forward+: Bringing Deferred Lighting to the Next Level". In: *Eurographics 2012 – Short Papers*. Ed. by Carlos Andujar

and Enrico Puppo. The Eurographics Association, 2012. DOI: https://doi.org/10.2312/conf/EG2012/short/005-008.

37. Kaiming He, Jian Sun, and Xiaoou Tang. "Guided Image Filtering". In: *IEEE Transactions on Pattern Analysis and Machine Intelligence* 35.6 (June 2013), pp. 1397–1409. ISSN: 0162-8828. DOI: https://doi.org/10.1109/TPAMI.2012.213.

38. Eric Heitz et al. "Real-time Polygonal-light Shading with Linearly Transformed Cosines". In: *ACM Transactions Graph.* 35.4 (July 2016), 41:1–41:8. ISSN: 0730-0301. DOI: https://doi.org/10.1145/2897824.2925895.

39. Peter Henry et al. "RGB-D Mapping: Using Depth Cameras for Dense 3D Modeling of Indoor Environments". In: *Experimental Robotics: The 12th International Symposium on Experimental Robotics.* Springer Berlin Heidelberg, 2014, pp. 477–491. DOI: https://doi.org/10.1007/978-3-642-28572-1_33.

40. Jan Herling and Wolfgang Broll. "High-Quality Real-Time Video Inpainting with PixMix". In: *IEEE Transactions on Visualization and Computer Graphics* 20.6 (June 2014), pp. 866–879. ISSN: 1077-2626. DOI: https://doi.org/10.1109/TVCG.2014.2298016.

41. Yannick Hold-Geoffroy, Akshaya Athawale, and Jean-Francois Lalonde. "Deep Sky-Modeling for Single Image Outdoor Lighting Estimation". In: *2019 IEEE Conference on Computer Vision and Pattern Recognition (CVPR).* IEEE, June 2019, pp. 6920–6928. DOI: https://doi.org/10.1109/CVPR.2019.00709.

42. Thomas Iorns and Taehyun Rhee. "Real-Time Image Based Lighting for 360-Degree Panoramic Video". In: *Image and Video Technology – PSIVT 2015 Workshops.* Ed. by Fay Huang and Sugimoto Akihiro. Vol. 9555. Springer International Publishing, 2016, pp. 139–151. ISBN: 9783319302843. DOI: https://doi.org/10.1007/978-3-319-30285-0_12.

43. Shahram Izadi et al. "KinectFusion: Real-time 3D Reconstruction and Interaction Using a Moving Depth Camera". In: Association for Computing Machinery (ACM), 2011, p. 559. ISBN: 9781450307161. DOI: https://doi.org/10.1145/2047196.2047270.

44. Jorge Jimenez et al. "SMAA: Enhanced Subpixel Morphological Antialiasing". In: *Computer Graphics Forum* 31.2pt1 (May 2012), pp. 355–364. DOI: https://doi.org/10.1111/j.1467-8659.2012.03014.x.

45. Olaf Kahler et al. "Very High Frame Rate Volumetric Integration of Depth Images on Mobile Devices". In: *IEEE Transactions on Visualization and Computer Graphics* 21.11 (Nov. 2015), pp. 1241–1250. ISSN: 1077-2626. DOI: https://doi.org/10.1109/TVCG.2015.2459891.

46. James T. Kajiya. "The Rendering Equation". In: *SIGGRAPH Comput. Graph.* 20.4 (Aug. 1986), pp. 143–150. ISSN: 0097-8930. DOI: https://doi.org/10.1145/15886.15902.

47. Pranoti Kale and K R Singh. "A Technical Analysis of Image Stitching Algorithm". In: *International Journal of Computer Science and Information Technologies (IJCSIT)* 6.1 (2015), pp. 284–288.

48. P. Kán and H. Kaufmann. "Differential Irradiance Caching for fast high-quality light transport between virtual and real worlds". In: *2013 IEEE International Symposium on Mixed and Augmented Reality (ISMAR).* Oct. 2013, pp. 133–141. DOI: https://doi.org/10.1109/ISMAR.2013.6671773.

49. Peter Kán and Hannes Kaufmann. "DeepLight: light source estimation for augmented reality using deep learning". In: *The Visual Computer* 35.6 (June 2019), pp. 873–883. ISSN: 1432-2315. DOI: https://doi.org/10.1007/s00371-019-01666-x.

50. Peter Kán, Johannes Unterguggenberger, and Hannes Kaufmann. "High- Quality Consistent Illumination in Mobile Augmented Reality by Radiance Convolution on the GPU". In: *Advances in Visual Computing: 11ᵗʰ International Symposium, ISVC 2015, Las Vegas, NV, USA, December 14–16, 2015, Proceedings, Part I*. Springer International Publishing, 2015, pp. 574–585. DOI: https://doi.org/10.1007/978-3-319-27857-5_52.

51. Anton Kaplanyan and Carsten Dachsbacher. "Cascaded light propagation volumes for real-time indirect illumination". In: *Proceedings of the ACM SIGGRAPH Symposium on Interactive 3D Graphics and Games – I3D 10*. Association for Computing Machinery (ACM), 2010. DOI: https://doi.org/10.1145/1730804.1730821.

52. Brian Karis. "Real Shading in Unreal Engine 4". In: *part of ACM SIGGRAPH 2013 Course: Physically Based Shading in Theory and Practice* (2013).

53. Kevin Karsch et al. "Automatic Scene Inference for 3D Object Compositing". In: *ACM Transactions on Graphics* 33.3 (June 2014), pp. 1–15. ISSN: 07300301. DOI: https://doi.org/10.1145/2602146.

54. Alexander Keller. "Instant radiosity". In: *Proceedings of the 24ᵗʰ annual conference on Computer graphics and interactive techniques SIGGRAPH 97* 31.3 (1997), pp. 49–56. ISSN: 00978930. DOI: https://doi.org/10.1145/258734.258769.

55. Maik Keller et al. "Real-time 3D Reconstruction in Dynamic Scenes using Point-based Fusion". In: *2013 International Conference on 3D Vision*. IEEE, June 2013, pp. 1–8. ISBN: 978-0-7695-5067-1. DOI: https://doi.org/10.1109/3DV.2013.9.

56. Christian Kerl, Jurgen Sturm, and Daniel Cremers. "Dense visual SLAM for RGB-D cameras". In: *2013 IEEE/RSJ International Conference on Intelligent Robots and Systems*. IEEE, Nov. 2013, pp. 2100–2106. DOI: https://doi.org/10.1109/IROS.2013.6696650.

57. J. Křivánek et al. "Radiance caching for efficient global illumination computation". In: *Visualization and Computer Graphics, IEEE Transactions on* 11.5 (Sept. 2005), pp. 550–561. ISSN: 1077-2626. DOI: https://doi.org/10.1109/TVCG.2005.83.

58. Jaroslav Křivánek and Mark Colbert. "Real-time Shading with Filtered Importance Sampling". In: *Computer Graphics Forum* 27.4 (June 2008), pp. 1147–1154. ISSN: 01677055. DOI: https://doi.org/10.1111/j.1467-8659.2008.01252.x.

59. Christian Kunert, Tobias Schwandt, and Wolfgang Broll. "An Efficient Diminished Reality Approach Using Real-Time Surface Reconstruction". In: *2019 International Conference on Cyberworlds (CW)*. Oct. 2019. DOI: https://doi.org/10.1109/CW.2019.00010.

60. Christian Kunert, Tobias Schwandt, and Wolfgang Broll. "Efficient Point Cloud Rasterization for Real Time Volumetric Integration in Mixed Reality Applications". In: *2018 IEEE International Symposium on Mixed and Augmented Reality (ISMAR)*. IEEE, 2018. DOI: https://doi.org/10.1109/ISMAR.2018.00023.

61. Sébastien Lagarde. Image-based Lighting approaches and parallax-corrected cubemap. 2012. URL: https://seblagarde.wordpress.com/2012/09/29/image-based-lighting-approaches-and-parallax-corrected-cubemap/ (visited on 08/30/2019).

62. Sébastien Lagarde and Charles De Rousiers. "Moving Frostbite to Physically Based Rendering". In: *part of ACM SIGGRAPH 2014 Course: Physically Based Shading in Theory and Practice* (2014).

63. Gilles Laurent et al. "Forward Light Cuts: A Scalable Approach to Real-Time Global Illumination". In: *Computer Graphics Forum* 35.4 (July 2016), pp. 79–88. DOI: https://doi.org/10.1111/cgf.12951.

64. Chloe LeGendre et al. "DeepLight: Learning Illumination for Unconstrained Mobile Mixed Reality". In: *2019 IEEE/CVF Conference on Computer Vision and Pattern Recognition (CVPR)*. IEEE, June 2019, pp. 5911–5921. DOI: https://doi.org/10.1109/CVPR.2019.00607.

65. Philipp Lensing. "LightSkin: Echtzeitbeleuchtung für Virtual und Augmented Reality". PhD thesis. Ilmenau University of Technology, 2014.

66. Philipp Lensing and Wolfgang Broll. "Fusing the real and the virtual: A depth-camera based approach to Mixed Reality". In: *2011 IEEE International Symposium on Mixed and Augmented Reality (ISMAR)*. IEEE, Oct. 2011, pp. 261–262. DOI: https://doi.org/10.1109/ISMAR.2011.6143892.

67. Philipp Lensing and Wolfgang Broll. "Instant indirect illumination for dynamic mixed reality scenes". In: *2012 IEEE International Symposium on Mixed and Augmented Reality (ISMAR)*. Institute of Electrical & Electronics Engineers (IEEE), Nov. 2012. DOI: https://doi.org/10.1109/ISMAR.2012.6402547.

68. Wei-Sheng Liao et al. "Real-Time Spherical Panorama Image Stitching Using OpenCL". In: *International Conference on Computer Graphics and Virtual Reality*. Las Vegas, America, July 2011.

69. Stephen Lombardi and Ko Nishino. "Reflectance and Natural Illumination from a Single Image". In: *Computer Vision – ECCV 2012*. Ed. by Andrew Fitzgibbon et al. Berlin, Heidelberg: Springer Berlin Heidelberg, 2012, pp. 582–595. ISBN: 978-3-642-33783-3.

70. Matthew M Loper and Michael J Black. "OpenDR: An approximate differentiable renderer". In: *European Conference on Computer Vision*. Springer. 2014, pp. 154–169.

71. Timothy Lottes. *FXAA*. https://developer.download.nvidia.com/assets/gamedev/files/sdk/11/FXAA_WhitePaper.pdf. 2009.

72. T.M. MacRobert. *Spherical Harmonics: An Elementary Treatise on Harmonic Functions, with Applications*. Chronic illness in the United States. Dover Publications, 1948.

73. David Mandl et al. "Learning Lightprobes for Mixed Reality Illumination". In: *2017 IEEE International Symposium on Mixed and Augmented Reality (ISMAR)*. IEEE, Oct. 2017. DOI: https://doi.org/10.1109/ISMAR.2017.25.

74. Steve Mann and Rosalind W Picard. "Virtual bellows: Constructing high quality stills from video". In: *Image Processing, 1994. Proceedings. ICIP-94., IEEE International Conference*. Vol. 1. IEEE. 1994, pp. 363–367.

75. Michael Mara et al. *Fast Global Illumination Approximations on Deep G-Buffers*. Tech. rep. NVR-2014-001. NVIDIA Corporation, June 2014.

76. Morgan McGuire and Michael Mara. "Efficient GPU Screen-Space Ray Tracing". In: *Journal of Computer Graphics Techniques (JCGT)* (2014), pp. 73–85.

77. Maxime Meilland and Andrew I. Comport. "On unifying key-frame and voxel-based dense visual SLAM at large scales". In: *2013 IEEE/RSJ International Conference on Intelligent Robots and Systems*. IEEE, Nov. 2013, pp. 3677–3683. DOI: https://doi.org/10.1109/IROS.2013.6696881.

78. Abhimitra Meka et al. "LIME: Live Intrinsic Material Estimation". In: *Proceedings of the IEEE Conference on Computer Vision and Pattern Recognition*. IEEE, June 2018, pp. 6315–6324. DOI: https://doi.org/10.1109/CVPR.2018.00661.

79. Abhimitra Meka et al. "Live intrinsic video". In: *ACM Transactions on Graphics* 35.4 (July 2016), pp. 1–14. DOI: https://doi.org/10.1145/2897824.2925907.

80. Paul Milgram et al. "Augmented Reality: A Class of Displays on the Reality-Virtuality Continuum". In: *Telemanipulator and Telepresence Technologies*. Ed. by Hari Das. SPIE, Dec. 1994, pp. 282–292. DOI: https://doi.org/10.1117/12.197321.

81. Shreyas Mistry and Arpita Patel. "Image Stitching using Harris Feature Detection Shreyas". In: *International Research Journal of Engineering and Technology (IRJET)* (2016).

82. Andreas Müller and Sarah Guido. *Introduction to Machine Learning with Python – A Guide for Data Scientists*. O'Reilly Media, Oct. 2016. ISBN: 9781449369415.

83. Oliver Nalbach, Tobias Ritschel, and Hans-Peter Seidel. "Deep screen space". In: *Proceedings of the 18th meeting of the ACM SIGGRAPH Symposium on Interactive 3D Graphics and Games – I3D '14*. Association for Computing Machinery (ACM), 2014, pp. 79–86. DOI: https://doi.org/10.1145/2556700.2556708.

84. R. A. Newcombe et al. "KinectFusion: Real-time dense surface mapping and tracking". In: *2011 IEEE International Symposium on Mixed and Augmented Reality ISMAR*. IEEE, Oct. 2011, pp. 127–136. DOI: https://doi.org/10.1109/ISMAR.2011.6092378.

85. Richard A. Newcombe, Steven J. Lovegrove, and Andrew J. Davison. "DTAM: Dense tracking and mapping in real-time". In: *2011 International Conference on Computer Vision*. IEEE, Nov. 2011, pp. 2320–2327. DOI: https://doi.org/10.1109/ICCV.2011.6126513.

86. Matthias Nießner et al. "Real-time 3D reconstruction at scale using voxel hashing". In: *ACM Transactions on Graphics* 32.6 (Nov. 2013), 169:1–169:11. ISSN: 0730-0301. DOI: https://doi.org/10.1145/2508363.2508374.

87. Ola Olsson, Markus Billeter, and Ulf Assarsson. "Clustered Deferred and Forward Shading". In: *Proceedings of the Fourth ACM SIGGRAPH / Eurographics Conference on High-Performance Graphics*. EGGH-HPG'12. Paris, France: Eurographics Association, 2012, pp. 87–96. ISBN: 978-3-905674-41-5. DOI: https://doi.org/10.2312/EGGH/HPG12/087-096.

88. Jinwoo Park et al. "Physically-inspired Deep Light Estimation from a Homogeneous-Material Object for Mixed Reality Lighting". In: *IEEE Transactions on Visualization and Computer Graphics* 26.5 (May 2020), pp. 2002–2011. DOI: https://doi.org/10.1109/TVCG.2020.2973050.

89. Deepak Pathak et al. "Context Encoders: Feature Learning by Inpainting". In: *2016 IEEE Conference on Computer Vision and Pattern Recognition (CVPR)*. IEEE, June 2016. DOI: https://doi.org/10.1109/CVPR.2016.278.

90. Ken Perlin. "An Image Synthesizer". In: *Proceedings of the 12th Annual Conference on Computer Graphics and Interactive Techniques*. SIGGRAPH '85. New York, NY, USA: Association for Computing Machinery, 1985, pp. 287–296. ISBN: 0897911660. DOI: https://doi.org/10.1145/325334.325247.

91. Matt Pharr, Wenzel Jakob, and Greg Humphreys. *Physically Based Rendering: From Theory to Implementation*. 3rd. San Francisco, CA, USA: Morgan Kaufmann Publishers Inc., 2016. ISBN: 9780128006450.

92. Bui Tuong Phong. "Illumination for Computer Generated Pictures". In: *Commun. ACM* 18.6 (June 1975), pp. 311–317. ISSN: 0001-0782. DOI: https://doi.org/10.1145/360825.360839.

93. E. Piazza, A. Romanoni, and M. Matteucci. "Real-Time CPU-Based Large-Scale Three-Dimensional Mesh Reconstruction". In: *IEEE Robotics and Automation Letters* 3.3 (July 2018), pp. 1584–1591. DOI: https://doi.org/10.1109/LRA.2018.2800104.

94. S. Pravenaa and R. Menaka. "A methodical review on image stitching and video stitching techniques". In: *International Journal of Applied Engineering Research* 11.5 (2016), pp. 3442–3448. ISSN: 09739769.

95. Ravi Ramamoorthi and Pat Hanrahan. "An Efficient Representation for Irradiance Environment Maps". In: *Proceedings of the 28th Annual Conference on Computer Graphics and Interactive Techniques*. SIGGRAPH '01. New York, NY, USA: ACM, 2001, pp. 497–500. ISBN: 1-58113-374-X. DOI: https://doi.org/10.1145/383259.383317.

96. Taehyun Rhee et al. "MR360: Mixed Reality Rendering for 360° Panoramic Videos". In: *IEEE Transactions on Visualization and Computer Graphics* 23.4 (Apr. 2017), pp. 1379–1388. DOI: https://doi.org/10.1109/TVCG.2017.2657178.

97. Thomas Richter-Trummer et al. "Instant Mixed Reality Lighting from Casual Scanning". In: *2016 IEEE International Symposium on Mixed and Augmented Reality (ISMAR)*. IEEE, Sept. 2016, pp. 27–36. DOI: https://doi.org/10.1109/ISMAR.2016.18.

98. T. Ritschel et al. "Imperfect shadow maps for efficient computation of indirect illumination". In: *ACM Transactions on Graphics* 27.5 (Dec. 2008), p. 1. DOI: https://doi.org/10.1145/1409060.1409082.

99. Tobias Ritschel et al. "The State of the Art in Interactive Global Illumination". In: *Comput. Graph. Forum* 31.1 (Feb. 2012), pp. 160–188. ISSN: 0167-7055. DOI: https://doi.org/10.1111/j.1467-8659.2012.02093.x.

100. Kai Rohmer et al. "Interactive Near-field Illumination for Photorealistic Augmented Reality on Mobile Devices". In: *2014 IEEE International Symposium on Mixed and Augmented Reality (ISMAR)*. IEEE, Sept. 2014, pp. 29–38. ISBN: 978-1-4799-6184-9. DOI: https://doi.org/10.1109/ISMAR.2014.6948406.

101. Timo Ropinski, Steffen Wachenfeld, and Klaus H Hinrichs. "Virtual Reflections for Augmented Reality Environments". In: *Proceedings of the 14th International Conference on Artificial Reality and Telexistence (ICAT04)* (2004), pp. 311–318.

102. Renato F. Salas-Moreno et al. "Dense planar SLAM". In: *2014 IEEE International Symposium on Mixed and Augmented Reality (ISMAR)*. IEEE, Sept. 2014, pp. 157–164. ISBN: 978-1-4799-6184-9. DOI: https://doi.org/10.1109/ISMAR.2014.6948422.

103. Renato F. Salas-Moreno et al. "SLAM++: Simultaneous localisation and mapping at the level of objects". In: IEEE, June 2013, pp. 1352–1359. ISBN: 978-0-7695-4989-7. DOI: https://doi.org/10.1109/CVPR.2013.178.

104. Christophe Schlick. "An Inexpensive BRDF Model for Physically-based Rendering". In: *Computer Graphics Forum* 13 (1994), pp. 233–246.

105. Thomas Schöps et al. "Large-scale outdoor 3D reconstruction on a mobile device". In: *Computer Vision and Image Understanding* 157 (Apr. 2017), pp. 151–166. DOI: https://doi.org/10.1016/j.CVIU.2016.09.007.

106. Tobias Schwandt and Wolfgang Broll. "A Single Camera Image Based Approach for Glossy Reflections in Mixed Reality Applications". In: *2016 IEEE International Sym-*

posium on Mixed and Augmented Reality (ISMAR). IEEE, 2016, pp. 37–43. DOI: https://doi.org/10.1109/ISMAR.2016.12.

107. Tobias Schwandt and Wolfgang Broll. "Differential G-Buffer Rendering for Mediated Reality Applications". In: *Augmented Reality, Virtual Reality, and Computer Graphics AVR 2017*. Ed. by Lucio Tommaso De Paolis, Patrick Bourdot, and Antonio Mongelli. Springer, Cham, June 2017, pp. 337–349. ISBN: 978-3-319-60928-7. DOI: https://doi.org/10.1007/978-3-319-60928-7_30.

108. Tobias Schwandt, Christian Kunert, and Wolfgang Broll. "Environment Estimation for Glossy Reflections in Mixed Reality Applications Using a Neural Network". In: *Transactions on Computational Science XXXVI: Special Issue on Cyberworlds and Cybersecurity*. Ed. by Marina L. Gavrilova, C.J. Kenneth Tan, and Alexei Sourin. Berlin, Heidelberg: Springer Berlin Heidelberg, 2020, pp. 26–42. ISBN: 978-3-662-61364-1. DOI: https://doi.org/10.1007/978-3-662-61364-1_2.

109. Tobias Schwandt, Christian Kunert, and Wolfgang Broll. "Glossy Reflections for Mixed Reality Environments on Mobile Devices". In: *International Conference on Cyberworlds*. IEEE, Oct. 2018, pp. 138–143. DOI: https://doi.org/10.1109/CW.2018.00034.

110. Shuran Song and Thomas Funkhouser. "Neural Illumination: Lighting Prediction for Indoor Environments". In: *2019 IEEE/CVF Conference on Computer Vision and Pattern Recognition (CVPR)*. IEEE, June 2019, pp. 6911–6919. DOI: https://doi.org/10.1109/CVPR.2019.00708.

111. Andrei State et al. "Superior augmented reality registration by integrating landmark tracking and magnetic tracking". In: *Proceedings of the 23rd annual conference on Computer graphics and interactive techniques SIGGRAPH 96* 30. Annual Conference Series (1996), pp. 429–438. ISSN: 0097-8930. DOI: https://doi.org/10.1145/237170.237282.

112. Richard Szeliski. "Image Alignment and Stitching: A Tutorial". In: *Foundations and Trends® in Computer Graphics and Vision* 2.1 (2006), pp. 1–104. ISSN: 1572-2740. DOI: https://doi.org/10.1561/0600000009.

113. Kostas Vardis, Georgios Papaioannou, and Anastasios Gkaravelis. "Realtime Radiance Caching using Chrominance Compression". In: *Journal of Computer Graphics Techniques (JCGT)* 3.4 (Dec. 2014), pp. 111–131. ISSN: 2331-7418.

114. Bruce Walter et al. "Microfacet Models for Refraction Through Rough Surfaces". In: *Proceedings of the 18th Eurographics Conference on Rendering Techniques*. EGSR'07. Grenoble, France: Eurographics Association, 2007, pp. 195–206. ISBN: 978-3-905673-52-4. DOI: https://doi.org/10.2312/EGWR/EGSR07/195-206.

115. Gregory J Ward, Francis M Rubinstein, and Robert D. Clear. "A ray tracing solution for diffuse interreflection". In: *ACM SIGGRAPH Computer Graphics* 22.4 (Aug. 1988), pp. 85–92. ISSN: 00978930. DOI: https://doi.org/10.1145/378456.378490.

116. T. Whelan et al. "Kintinuous: Spatially Extended KinectFusion". In: *RSS Workshop on RGB-D: Advanced Reasoning with Depth Cameras*. 2012, pp. 1–8.

117. Thomas Whelan et al. "ElasticFusion: Dense SLAM Without A Pose Graph". In: *Robotics: Science and Systems XI*. Rome, Italy: Robotics: Science and Systems Foundation, July 2015. DOI: https://doi.org/10.15607/RSS.2015.XI.001.

118. Thomas Whelan et al. "Incremental and batch planar simplification of dense point cloud maps". In: *Robotics and Autonomous Systems* 69 (Jan. 2014), pp. 3–14. DOI: https://doi.org/10.1016/j.robot.2014.08.019.

119. Shihao Wu et al. "Specular-to-Diffuse Translation for Multi-view Reconstruction". In: *ECCV*. Springer International Publishing, 2018, pp. 193–211. DOI: https://doi.org/10. 1007/978-3-030-01225-0_12.

120. Jianxiong Xiao et al. "Recognizing scene viewpoint using panoramic place representation". In: *Proceedings of the IEEE Computer Society Conference on Computer Vision and Pattern Recognition* (2012), pp. 2695–2702. ISSN: 10636919. DOI: https://doi.org/ 10.1109/CVPR.2012.6247991.

121. Jinsong Zhang et al. "All-Weather Deep Outdoor Lighting Estimation". In: *2019 IEEE/CVF Conference on Computer Vision and Pattern Recognition (CVPR)*. IEEE, June 2019, pp. 10150–10158. DOI: https://doi.org/10.1109/CVPR.2019.01040.

122. Yizhong Zhang et al. "Online Structure Analysis for Real-Time Indoor Scene Reconstruction". In: *ACM Transactions on Graphics* 34.5 (Nov. 2015), 159:1–159:13. ISSN: 0730-0301. DOI: https://doi.org/10.1145/2768821.

123. Qian-Yi Zhou and Vladlen Koltun. "Dense scene reconstruction with points of interest". In: *ACM Transactions on Graphics* 32.4 (July 2013), 112:1–112:8. DOI: https://doi.org/ 10.1145/2461912.2461919.

124. Qian-Yi Zhou, Stephen Miller, and Vladlen Koltun. "Elastic Fragments for Dense Scene Reconstruction". In: *2013 IEEE International Conference on Computer Vision*. IEEE, Dec. 2013. DOI: https://doi.org/10.1109/ICCV.2013.65.

119. Shihao Wu et al. "Specular-to Diffuse Translation for Multi-view Reconstruction". In: *ECCV*. Springer International Publishing, 2018, pp. 193–211. DOI: https://doi.org/10.1007/978-3-030-01225-0_12.

120. Jianxiong Xiao et al. "Recognizing scene viewpoint using panoramic place representation". In: *Proceedings of the IEEE Computer Society Conference on Computer Vision and Pattern Recognition* (2012), pp. 2695–2702. ISSN: 10636919. DOI: https://doi.org/10.1109/CVPR.2012.6247991.

121. Jinsong Zhang et al. "All-Weather Deep Outdoor Lighting Estimation". In: *2019 IEEE/CVF Conference on Computer Vision and Pattern Recognition (CVPR)*. IEEE, June 2019, pp. 10150–10158. DOI: https://doi.org/10.1109/CVPR.2019.01040.

122. Yizhong Zhang et al. "Online Structure Analysis for Real-Time Indoor Scene Reconstruction". In: *ACM Transactions on Graphics* 34.5 (Nov. 2015), 159:1–159:13. ISSN: 0730-0301. DOI: https://doi.org/10.1145/2768821.

123. Qian-Yi Zhou and Vladlen Koltun. "Dense scene reconstruction with points of interest". In: *ACM Transactions on Graphics* 32.4 (July 2013), 112:1–112:8. DOI: https://doi.org/10.1145/2461912.2461919.

124. Qian-Yi Zhou, Stephen Miller, and Vladlen Koltun. "Elastic Fragments for Dense Scene Reconstruction". In: *2013 IEEE International Conference on Computer Vision*. IEEE, Dec. 2013. DOI: https://doi.org/10.1109/ICCV.2013.65.

posium on Mixed and Augmented Reality (ISMAR). IEEE, 2016, pp. 37–43. DOI: https://doi.org/10.1109/ISMAR.2016.12.

107. Tobias Schwandt and Wolfgang Broll. "Differential G-Buffer Rendering for Mediated Reality Applications". In: *Augmented Reality, Virtual Reality, and Computer Graphics AVR 2017*. Ed. by Lucio Tommaso De Paolis, Patrick Bourdot, and Antonio Mongelli. Springer, Cham, June 2017, pp. 337–349. ISBN: 978-3-319-60928-7. DOI: https://doi.org/10.1007/978-3-319-60928-7_30.

108. Tobias Schwandt, Christian Kunert, and Wolfgang Broll. "Environment Estimation for Glossy Reflections in Mixed Reality Applications Using a Neural Network". In: *Transactions on Computational Science XXXVI: Special Issue on Cyberworlds and Cybersecurity*. Ed. by Marina L. Gavrilova, C.J. Kenneth Tan, and Alexei Sourin. Berlin, Heidelberg: Springer Berlin Heidelberg, 2020, pp. 26–42. ISBN: 978-3-662-61364-1. DOI: https://doi.org/10.1007/978-3-662-61364-1_2.

109. Tobias Schwandt, Christian Kunert, and Wolfgang Broll. "Glossy Reflections for Mixed Reality Environments on Mobile Devices". In: *International Conference on Cyberworlds*. IEEE, Oct. 2018, pp. 138–143. DOI: https://doi.org/10.1109/CW.2018.00034.

110. Shuran Song and Thomas Funkhouser. "Neural Illumination: Lighting Prediction for Indoor Environments". In: *2019 IEEE/CVF Conference on Computer Vision and Pattern Recognition (CVPR)*. IEEE, June 2019, pp. 6911–6919. DOI: https://doi.org/10.1109/CVPR.2019.00708.

111. Andrei State et al. "Superior augmented reality registration by integrating landmark tracking and magnetic tracking". In: *Proceedings of the 23rd annual conference on Computer graphics and interactive techniques SIGGRAPH 96* 30. Annual Conference Series (1996), pp. 429–438. ISSN: 0097-8930. DOI: https://doi.org/10.1145/237170.237282.

112. Richard Szeliski. "Image Alignment and Stitching: A Tutorial". In: *Foundations and Trends® in Computer Graphics and Vision* 2.1 (2006), pp. 1–104. ISSN: 1572-2740. DOI: https://doi.org/10.1561/0600000009.

113. Kostas Vardis, Georgios Papaioannou, and Anastasios Gkaravelis. "Realtime Radiance Caching using Chrominance Compression". In: *Journal of Computer Graphics Techniques (JCGT)* 3.4 (Dec. 2014), pp. 111–131. ISSN: 2331-7418.

114. Bruce Walter et al. "Microfacet Models for Refraction Through Rough Surfaces". In: *Proceedings of the 18th Eurographics Conference on Rendering Techniques*. EGSR'07. Grenoble, France: Eurographics Association, 2007, pp. 195–206. ISBN: 978-3-905673-52-4. DOI: https://doi.org/10.2312/EGWR/EGSR07/195-206.

115. Gregory J Ward, Francis M Rubinstein, and Robert D. Clear. "A ray tracing solution for diffuse interreflection". In: *ACM SIGGRAPH Computer Graphics* 22.4 (Aug. 1988), pp. 85–92. ISSN: 00978930. DOI: https://doi.org/10.1145/378456.378490.

116. T. Whelan et al. "Kintinuous: Spatially Extended KinectFusion". In: *RSS Workshop on RGB-D: Advanced Reasoning with Depth Cameras*. 2012, pp. 1–8.

117. Thomas Whelan et al. "ElasticFusion: Dense SLAM Without A Pose Graph". In: *Robotics: Science and Systems XI*. Rome, Italy: Robotics: Science and Systems Foundation, July 2015. DOI: https://doi.org/10.15607/RSS.2015.XI.001.

118. Thomas Whelan et al. "Incremental and batch planar simplification of dense point cloud maps". In: *Robotics and Autonomous Systems* 69 (Jan. 2014), pp. 3–14. DOI: https://doi.org/10.1016/j.robot.2014.08.019.

Printed in the United States
by Baker & Taylor Publisher Services